Additional Praise for *The Customer Learning Curve: Creating Profits from Marketing Chaos*

"*The Customer Learning Curve* has two big advantages over most books on marketing. First, it takes the whole marketing task into consideration—not just advertising, not just sales, not just customer service, but the whole process. The second advantage is that it provides a road map for finding the right numbers and crunching them. Spreadsheets made it easy to crunch numbers, the Internet made it easy to find numbers, and now Hellman and Burst make it easy to put the two together so that a reasonably thoughtful practitioner can do the right analysis with the right data. This book should be on the bookshelf of anyone who has a task such as 'prepare annual marketing plan' on their To Do list."

—Steven Whitelaw, Principal, Whitelaw & Co.

"The beauty of *The Customer Learning Curve* is that it helps marketers quickly focus on the highest leverage activities. Start with the facts you have, and use the discipline of the CLC model to estimate those you don't have. These estimates help you make priority decisions consistent with your information and your judgments. The estimates become hypotheses to test with market research and marketing experience."

—Frank Grillo, Senior Vice President, Marketing, Z-Tel

"As part of providing world-class service, we are always looking for state-of-the-art management ideas to share with our clients. *The Customer Learning Curve* has been very well received by senior executives who want to focus their organizations on their customers and win and keep customers in the most efficient way."

—Juan Carlos Lopez Vives, Managing Director,
Bearing Point, España

"During times of change, strategic marketers are faced with a combination of too much new information and the chaos of trying to organize the information usefully. *The Customer Learning Curve* provides a framework for sorting through and making sense of the overwhelming amount of information available today. Getting information is not the problem; it is understanding it and taking correct action in these disruptive situations that is the challenge."

—Garry Betty, President, Earthlink

"*The Customer Learning Curve* is an important contribution to the emerging thinking on how to deal with new market realities. It can help the beginner perform the fundamental tasks better, and it can help the experienced master create masterpieces. Read this book and make the effort to use its tools. It is certain to improve your company's marketing ROI."

—From the Foreword by Frank V. Cespedes, author of *Concurrent Marketing*, and Managing Partner, The Center for Executive Development

THE
Customer
Learning
Curve

CREATING PROFITS
FROM MARKETING CHAOS

THE
Customer
Learning
Curve

CREATING PROFITS FROM
MARKETING CHAOS

KARL HELLMAN   ARDIS BURST

Australia · Canada · Mexico · Singapore · Spain · United Kingdom · United States

THOMSON
™
SOUTH-WESTERN

The Customer Learning Curve: Creating Profits from Marketing Chaos
Karl Hellman and Ardis Burst

Vice President/
Editorial Director
Jack Calhoun

Vice President/
Editor-in-Chief
Dave Shaut

Acquisition Editor
Steve Momper

Channel Manager,
Retail
Chris McNamee

Channel Manager,
Professional
Mark Linton

Production Manager
Tricia Matthews Boies

Production Editor
Alan Biondi

Manufacturing Coordinator
Charlene Taylor

Cover Design
Jeanne Nemcek

Design and Composition
Mary Loye

Design Project Manager
Rik Moore

Compositor
American Marketing
Association

Printer
Edwards Brothers, Inc.
Lillington, NC

AMA Director of Publications
Francesca Van Gorp Cooley

International Division List

ASIA (Including India):
Thomson Learning
60 Albert Street, #15-01
Albert Complex
Singapore 189969
Tel 65 336-6411
Fax 65 336-7411

AUSTRALIA/NEW ZEALAND:
Nelson
102 Dodds Street
South Melbourne
Victoria 3205
Australia
Tel 61 (0)3 9685-4111
Fax 61 (0)3 9685-4199

LATIN AMERICA:
Thomson Learning
Seneca 53
Colonia Polanco
11560 Mexico, D.F. Mexico
Tel (525) 281-2906
Fax (525) 281-2656

CANADA:
Nelson
1120 Birchmount Road
Toronto, Ontario
Canada M1K 5G4
Tel (416) 752-9100
Fax (416) 752-8102

UK/EUROPE/MIDDLE EAST/
AFRICA:
Thomson Learning
Berkshire House
168-173 High Holborn
London WC1V 7AA
United Kingdom
Tel 44 (0)20 497-1422
Fax 44 (0)20 497-1426

SPAIN (includes Portugal):
Paraninfo
Calle Magallanes 25
28015 Madrid
España
Tel 34 (0)91 446-3350
Fax 34 (0)91 445-6218

To Donna, Catherine, Christopher, and Matthew
in appreciation for their love, patience,
encouragement, and support.

—KARL HELLMAN

To Katie and Richard, my angels.

—ARDIS BURST

Table of Contents

Foreword

During the past decade, the context for planning and implementing marketing activities has changed dramatically, especially in business-to-business (B2B) exchanges. The supply chain revolution, online channels, Web exchanges, and a new emphasis by companies on more rigorous management of working capital have altered both the external environment that marketers face and the internal analytical and organizational requirements for effective marketing.

As always, disruptive change means opportunities as well as threats, and the need for a comprehensive but practical framework is essential. *The Customer Learning Curve* provides strategists with an excellent start to the process of discovering the key building blocks required to make sense of new realities and so focus on the high-leverage issues and opportunities. The book is a unique tool for developing insights into customer buying decisions and presents a financial model for determining key marketing leverage points and investment decisions.

As does all enduring advice about marketing, this book focuses on the customer, but it is particularly relevant to B2B practitioners for several reasons. First, *The Customer Learning Curve* addresses the distinguishing reality of B2B markets. As opposed to media advertising, merchandising, or other staples of consumer marketing wisdom, a spectrum of pre- and postpurchase activities is typically more important to B2B marketing efforts because of multiple tiers of distribution and the need to align applications and offerings with multiple customers.

Second, new techniques and metrics (e.g., activity-based costing, value-based management) make more visible the way differences in buying behavior affect the transaction costs and (un)profitability of customer groups. Customer relationship management technologies provide a means to identify, track, and manage these differences, but without a shared understanding of the customer learning process and purchase dynamics, the millions now being spent on these initiatives will have a limited and even counterproductive effect. An implicit but important theme in this book is that no amount of technology can substitute for this understanding.

Third, precisely because of the complexity of technologies and marketing tasks, too many B2B companies fragment their learning about customers across different functions and departments at a time when marketing activities require coordination. In my book *Concurrent Marketing: Integrating Product, Sales, and Service* (Harvard Business School Press, 1995), I discuss this common misfit between market developments and organizational capabilities. Product, sales, and service units must synchronize their efforts to deliver value to customers, but over time each unit adopts routines that improve the efficiency of its particular responsibilities. Too often the result is a series of disabling "competency traps": Each group becomes better at "fighting the last war"—executing marketing programs relevant to a previous stage of competition—but unwittingly hampers the company's ability to deal with changing market conditions.

By adopting a comprehensive, customer-centric perspective across the purchase process, *The Customer Learning Curve* provides a managerial tool for aligning internal operations with external opportunities. This increases the ability of companies to learn not only about customers, and so implement profitable concurrent marketing initiatives, but also from customers, and so truly initiate continuous improvement in marketing and management activities.

The Customer Learning Curve is an important contribution to the emerging thinking on how to deal with new market realities. It can help the beginner perform the fundamental tasks better, and it can help the experienced master create masterpieces. Read this book and make the effort to use its tools. It is certain to improve your company's marketing ROI.

Frank V. Cespedes
Managing Partner
The Center for Executive Development
Boston, Mass.

Chapter 1

Marketing Chaos, and What to Do About It

As we move into the twenty-first century, business-to-business marketing is being turned upside down, inside out, and sideways. Recent crises include dealing with e-commerce and economic downturns, but crisis itself is nothing new. Fallout from ever-larger mergers and acquisitions, the effect of flattened organizations and "streamlined" staff, globalization of suppliers and customers, and accelerating technological change are challenges that can keep the most skillful business-to-business marketing manager awake long into the night.

Each change amplifies the effect of another, and the almost chaotic situations that result do not lend themselves to simple answers. One more analytic model or set of "self-help" guidelines can address only parts of the problems. What companies really need is a method for understanding complex challenges at a deeper level—a level that reaches beyond *today's* crisis. The Customer Learning Curve (CLC) is that method. With the CLC, you can ferret out the most important problems your company faces, pinpoint your best opportunities, and develop insights into how to forge success, quarter after quarter and year after year. The CLC suggests intelligent questions to ask about what a company accepts as conventional wisdom.

Our approach is grounded in years of research and consulting with business-to-business and consumer goods companies, which have consistently achieved breakthrough results from their CLC-guided marketing efforts. This book will give you the information you need to join these marketing success stories, to make the CLC work for *your* business.

HOW CAN YOU USE THE CUSTOMER LEARNING CURVE?

In the office of almost every marketing manager in the country, there is a shelf full of books with wonderful ideas for improving business. Most have been read an average of .2 times and must be dusted regularly by the cleaning team. This book is not likely to meet that fate. Why? *The Customer Learning Curve* offers a perspective that you can put into practice immediately, and it provides new ideas and approaches that will continue to build your business well into the future. The following are just some of the benefits that *The Customer Learning Curve* will help you achieve in your company.

Everyone Develops a Marketing Perspective

In most companies, not everyone who has marketing responsibility has a well-developed and sharply honed set of marketing skills. For example, the managers at Dunamis, an Atlanta educational software company, were experts in software development but had virtually no marketing training. Suddenly they were faced with marketing chaos: Despite success stories, testimonials, and happy clients, the company badly needed to increase sales and profits.

How could the Dunamis managers figure out what to do first, next, and next again? Using the questions suggested by the CLC approach, they broke their problems into discrete components and developed a clear understanding of how to use marketing to address each issue.

Even if most marketing managers in your organization are skilled, there are always newcomers or marketers who enter from other disciplines or functional areas of the company. The CLC model can help them develop a perspective on products or services that will greatly strengthen their marketing contributions.

Cope with Too Many Choices

One product group at a major telecommunications company used the CLC model to develop a marketing plan. They were comfortable with the "go forward" model they designed after plugging in their hard numbers and fine-tuning the estimates of the CLC Web tool (discussed later). They had even chosen three steps of the CLC in which to intervene, but they were stymied by how to create and cost out good new program ideas.

Each group member searched for relevant information and came up with nothing. Finally, the most junior person was given the assignment of checking with the market research department one last time, to make sure there was no useful information in the archives. His findings? Hidden away were half a dozen relevant studies, all less than two years old. Suddenly, the information gap became a deluge, and the group had to choose among too many options.

At this point, the product group might have struggled for months to make choices and might have ended up with a program whose performance was less than optimal. Instead, they returned to the CLC model to evaluate the ideas that these studies generated. After selecting the best candidates, the group compared options and came up with a set of programs that ultimately raised sales and profits substantially. Faced with too many choices, the group used the CLC approach to pinpoint what was important and where to take action.

Deal Effectively with Disruption

Marketplace disruption can come in many forms. There are technological disruptions, such as the rapid, ongoing changes that characterize the computer industry. There are communications disruptions, most recently fueled by the spread of Internet usage. There are logistical disruptions: overnight package delivery or airline hub systems. There are product life cycle disruptions, when an entire industry may spring into being or decline precipitously in a matter of months. Almost always, these disruptions are accompanied by a flood of new information.

Garry Betty, President of Earthlink, describes the usefulness of the CLC method to deal with the disruptions that his company faces almost routinely. "During times of change, strategic marketers are faced with a combination of too much new information and the chaos of trying to organize the information usefully. The Customer Learning Curve provides a framework for sorting through and making sense out of the overwhelming amount of information available today. Getting information is not the problem. It's understanding it and taking correct action in these disruptive situations that is the challenge."

Make Midcourse Corrections

One product group in a major food manufacturing company needed to respond to a competitive advertising assault in the middle of the planning year. Annual budgets had been established months before. Now the group believed it needed to invest an extra $1 million in powerful and convincing new campaigns to defend its position in the marketplace in the face of much higher advertising expenditures by the competitor.

A team at a regional telecommunications company was in an even worse situation. The team was formed in a midyear corporate restructuring, too late to present any marketing plan at all. There was no budget, no money for market research, no access to marketing program resources, and no data from the corporate accounting system to help the team propose expenditures to top management. All members knew was that their share of a market worth $250 million annually was less than 1%. This share had been almost solely generated by a direct mail piece that was sent to customers when the product was part of another group. The newly structured marketing team believed that $4 million spent wisely could increase sales to more than $30 million, but it had no leverage to ask for the budget.

How could these two groups of marketing managers make a case for funding their products? In both situations, they used the CLC model to perform a kind of sensitivity analysis of their two options: Do nothing or implement a program.

The food products group investigated what would happen if the competitor's advertisements reduced their current sales. It was estimated that a loss of only 4% of volume would reduce profit contribution more than the $1 million they wanted to invest. They demonstrated that if no action was taken, the parent company would likely suffer losses greater than the costs of additional advertising. Furthermore, the product would enter the next planning year with even lower market share, which would require even more advertising investments in the future.

The telecommunications group used the CLC model in a similar way. They began by brainstorming specific programs that were likely to increase volume, costed these programs out, and estimated their effect on total sales and profit contribution. This was the "most likely" business case, and the model was rerun to show "best" and "worst" case scenarios. Even in the worst scenario, the parent company would benefit substantially from investing in the product group's programs. When the marketing team went to top management with such clear support for the proposals, management found the money, and the group went forward with their plans before year end.

The CLC model can open discussion regarding the kinds of course changes needed. If your company needs to make mid-course corrections or overcome the hurdle of limited resources, the CLC approach can definitely help.

Assess the Progress of a New Product or Service

It is risky to wait for internal systems to evaluate the progress of a new product. Bad news can come too late, and when it does arrive, you typically will not know what problems need to be fixed. The CLC tells you what to measure to assess progress. It will help you know whether to ask about target market awareness, distribution, customer perceptions of product value, or something altogether different.

Update What You "Know"

The CLC suggests intelligent questions to ask about what a company accepts as conventional wisdom. For example, many companies believe that the task of building awareness is complete when buyers know their product exists. The Next Day Air SM delivery service product teams at United Parcel Service understood that just because 90% of their target market knew about their service, that did not mean customers would choose it over the competition. Yes, they measured awareness of the service, but they also asked customers about reasons for choosing UPS over other service providers.

When setting up the CLC model, the Next Day Air team input 90% (the proportion of the target aware of the service) in the awareness step, then inserted all the other numbers they had available. The final calculation revealed that sales volume should be much higher. The conclusion? The appropriate figure to use, the lower number, consisted of those who could cite a reason for using Next Day Air. When this lower percentage was used in the awareness step, predicted sales were in line with actual experience. The team then focused on developing programs to educate users about points-of-difference services and thereby increased sales and profits.

Perhaps your company has competing truths. (At UPS, one "truth" was that 90% of prospects knew about the service, and the other "truth" was that a smaller proportion had a compelling reason to use it.) Or perhaps there are things that everyone in the company "knows" are true ("Our customers aren't interested in buying products online") but that no longer make sense. (You have lost 25% of your share of market, while your major competitor has pushed hard for online selling, with a sophisticated Web site and customer support function, and has gained 25%.) The CLC provides an objective way to look at these truths, so you can avoid the battle of opinion that often creates strife rather than improves the business.

Help Top Management Make Good Choices

In the interactive reality of most companies, products or services vie for scarce dollar resources. This creates frustrations on all sides of the discussion. Talented strategic marketers have a hard time justifying their "gut feeling" about why funds should be invested in a certain program, and top management finds it difficult to make "rational" choices about allocations.

The CLC levels the playing field for these evaluations. It enables top management to make realistic comparisons and choose which products or services to support. According to David Kennedy, former general manager of Coca-Cola's Fountain Division, the CLC method "translates the intuition of the professional marketer into the dollars and cents language of the general managers who have to make investment decisions."

At the same time, the CLC supports the professional marketer's intuition with realistic number projections. David Bridges, a marketing consultant at Georgia Tech University, says: "When I was a product manager, I always *knew* I had good marketing programs. I had research and analysis that told me I had developed good programs. But there was always one question from management I could never answer: 'How do you know there is not *another* program that would give us a better return?' The CLC provides the answer to that question."

THE CUSTOMER LEARNING CURVE APPROACH

The CLC is a unique tool with two robust components: a technique for developing deep insight into customer decision making and a practical financial model to determine marketing leverage points and the returns on alternative marketing expenditures.

Traditionally, the term "learning curve" refers to the phenomenon that repetition enhances performance. The very first time a player serves a tennis ball, a lot of effort is required, and the ball is often out of bounds. But the thousandth serve is usually relatively effortless and often results in a well-placed shot. The concept of the learning curve is well established in management: It was first described by Wright (1936) in an article on ways to improve airplane assembly.[1] The customer learning curve refers to a continuum that ranges from knowing nothing about a product or service to being a loyal, repeat user.

Many companies, particularly in business-to-business settings, do not have a consistent, strong model for understanding customers. Their approach is piecemeal because various departments within the company look at things differently, and no one consistently integrates their observations. Engineers consider what technology customers want, the sales force is concerned about price sensitivity, and customer service representatives know about problems related to products and services. Meanwhile, the marketing department focuses on creating memorable advertising campaigns or trade promotions to increase distribution and sales volume. From the point of view of the customer, these components—technology, price, service, communications, and distribution—are parts of a whole, an integrated bundle of benefits. The process of learning about, deciding to buy, purchasing, and using a product or service is a single continuum; the selling company's organizational division of labor is irrelevant.

By looking at every aspect of selling a product or service from the customer's point of view, the CLC method forces a company to take an integrated, customer-centered approach. This approach guarantees that the marketers themselves will also move through a learning curve, which improves both their understanding of customers and their effectiveness in reaching them.

Component One: Customer Insight

The CLC's power to help business-to-business marketers improve performance comes from its core insight: The marketing process that matters most happens in the customer's mind. Whether this decision maker is an individual or a committee charged with choosing a product or service, the process is the same. Potential buyers must *learn* that they need what you are selling, where to find it, how to buy and use it, and how to expe-

---

[1]Wright (1936) discusses the learning curve concept and provides guidelines for estimating the impact of learning curves on manufacturing processes.

rience value from it. The result of successful marketing is customer learning.

Many marketing tasks are required to facilitate and support customer learning: advertising, research, promotion, product development, public relations, packaging, and more. One business-to-business company, for example, identified 110 discrete marketing tasks that were woven into more than a dozen internal business processes. Unfortunately, successfully working through each of these disjointed tasks did not improve bottom-line results. The company achieved little business leverage and enjoyed no measurable sales lift, no matter how much improvement was made in each of these individual marketing activities.

Using the CLC perspective, this company revised its approach and thought about the 110 activities from the customer's point of view. Specific activities were clustered to help customers learn what they needed to know, so that they moved along the curve toward purchase and repurchase. The company not only increased sales and profits substantially but also built the kind of customer loyalty it had been seeking for years.

Plotting the CLC

Imagine that a business-to-business company has a great product or service, the best available in some applications or perhaps even in all applications. Before the company can succeed, potential customers must learn why, where, how, and when to become a customer.

- Prospects must need the product or service and learn that they need it.
  No **need** means no customer.
- Prospects who need the product or service must become aware of why they should purchase from a particular company.
  No **awareness** means no customer.
- Prospects aware of the product or service must learn where to find it.
  No **access** means no customer.
- Prospects who can find the product or service need a compelling reason to buy it.
  No **motivation** means no customer.
- Motivated prospects must then buy the product or service.
  No **purchase** means no customer.

If a prospect stays on the learning curve until a sale is made, traditional business-to-business marketing often views this as success, the end of the story. But from the customer's point of view, the total learning process is far from complete.

The Customer Learning Curve Does Not End with a Purchase

Is a purchaser a customer? Many marketers think so. They feel satisfied that money has been spent on what they are selling, which is indeed a critical point. Yet the customer-centered view of the CLC does not end with purchase. Recall that the marketing process that matters most happens in the customer's mind.

■ Purchasers must learn to use the product or service.
No proper **use** means no loyal, repeat customer.
■ Purchasers who learn to use the product or service must experience value, that is, believe they received the benefits they expected and that the benefits were worth the price.
No **value experienced** means no loyal, repeat customer.
■ Purchasers who experience value must still be cared for and perhaps given extra incentives to remain continuous, loyal customers.
No **loyalty** means the company must start all over again with this customer.

When a purchaser continues to buy and use a product or service, tells colleagues to use it, and becomes a friend of the firm, then and only then does the business-to-business company have a true customer.

Because moving a customer from needing what you sell to being a loyal user is such a complex process, selling a business-to-business product or service is never an easy proposition. Someone must make it all work. Someone must use the CLC approach to spot the points at which potential customers run the risk of not moving forward and design programs to get prospects past those barriers. That person becomes not just a regular marketer, charged with maximizing performance in one or another step of the CLC or in one particular aspect of developing the marketing mix, but a strategic marketer whose perspective constantly encompasses the continuum of actions that create a loyal customer.

The strategic marketer may be a product manager, a category manager, a marketing vice president, or even a chief executive officer or company owner. Regardless of title, this is the person who takes responsibility for keeping the entire CLC in mind as he or she evaluates and manages marketing activities. (We discuss the role and identity of the strategic marketer in more depth near the end of Chapter 2.) For the strategic marketer, each step of the CLC approach raises specific strategic questions.

- Step One: "Exactly who needs my product or service, and do they already know they need it?"
- Step Two: "Who is aware not only of my product or service but also of its potential benefits for them as users?"
- Step Three: "Who has access to what I am selling?" This can be especially important in service industries.
- Step Four: "What does it take to motivate people to want to buy my product or service?"
- Step Five: "What does it take to generate purchase?"
- Step Six: "What is involved in teaching my customer to learn how to use my product or service effectively?"
- Step Seven: "How can I make sure that my customers experience value after they buy and learn to use what I am selling?"
- Step Eight: "What actions are necessary to create loyal users or to generate repurchase of my product or service?"

Component Two: Financial Model

The CLC financial model enables the strategic marketer to select the best marketing program, defined as the one that increases revenue the most per dollar of marketing expenditures. This selection process is central to the second component of the CLC.

Business-to-business marketing strategies and programs usually evolve without a strong, customer-centered framework against which to evaluate them. Consequently, marketing managers may find it difficult to assess one program versus another. The eight steps of the CLC provide a sort of gateway through which prospects must pass. (The easiest way to see how the math works is to access the CLC model at the Web site, www.resultrek.com, by clicking on "The Customer Learning Curve Model." Just follow the directions.)

The following text and charts describe how the CLC works: Suppose you learn through market research that half the companies in a particular industry or geographic territory need your product and that the total number of prospects in that target market is 4000. Therefore, the maximum number of possible customers is 2000.

Market research also tells you that only 40% of those who need your product are aware it even exists. If Need = 50% and

Aware = 40%, maximum penetration is figured at 50% × 40%, or 20% of 4000, which is 800. (Another way to see how the math works is to access the Web site, www.resultrek.com, and click on "The Customer Learning Curve Model.")

Exhibit 1-1 shows the numbers already discussed as well as values for the percentage of prospects who make it through each of the next six CLC steps. Multiply the percentages together to determine penetration, or the number of customers who make it through all the stages.

You are left with only 40 customers in this target market, 1% of the original audience, who can be considered loyal customers; the rest drop out during the progression from Need to Retain. What should you do? The CLC provides a way to determine both where to intervene in this customer-education process and which programs to implement to improve performance.

In the CLC model, each marketing program has a specific numerical objective: to raise the percentage of "throughput" in one or more of the CLC's steps. Exhibit 1-2 shows the effect of two initiatives with specific throughput targets: an advertising program to increase awareness from 40% to 60% and a sales training and incentive program to raise the close (purchase) rate from 50% to 75%. The result of these two interventions was that sales more than doubled!

Now imagine a more complex situation, typical of those that confront business-to-business strategic marketers every day. Samantha Hathaway, Vice President of Marketing for Aries

EXHIBIT 1-1
How the Customer Learning Curve Numbers Work

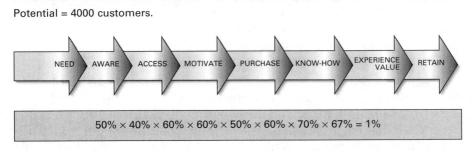

Potential = 4000 customers.

NEED AWARE ACCESS MOTIVATE PURCHASE KNOW-HOW EXPERIENCE VALUE RETAIN

50% × 40% × 60% × 60% × 50% × 60% × 70% × 67% = 1%

Penetration = 40 customers.

EXHIBIT 1-2
Effect of Changes in the Customer Learning Curve

Potential = 4000 customers.

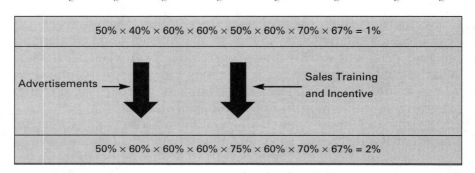

NEED | AWARE | ACCESS | MOTIVATE | PURCHASE | KNOW-HOW | EXPERIENCE VALUE | RETAIN

50% × 40% × 60% × 60% × 50% × 60% × 70% × 67% = 1%

Advertisements →

Sales Training and Incentive

50% × 60% × 60% × 60% × 75% × 60% × 70% × 67% = 2%

Penetration = 40 customers.

85 customers.

Software, a hypothetical Silicon Valley company, is facing too many marketing options. To double sales, should she add sales-people, which has worked in the past, or spend more money on advertising? The company's hot-shot advertising agency has just presented a brilliant campaign idea with high recall among potential software buyers. Or perhaps Aries should reengineer its software to integrate new user-friendly features suggested by the product development department.

The CLC provides Hathaway with a way to make an informed and profit-maximizing choice. By working through the eight steps that describe how customers make decisions, she can identify exactly where her prospects need support. If the product already has a high level of awareness among customers, for example, investment in advertising may not be the answer. By organizing insights about Aries customers, the CLC will point Hathaway in the right strategic marketing direction, as illustrated in Exhibit 1-3.

EXHIBIT 1-3
Aries Software's Customer Learning Curve

Potential = 400,000 customers.

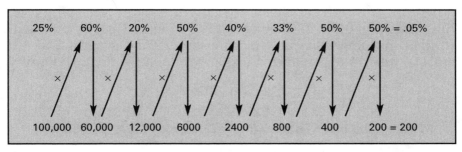

Penetration = 200 customers.

An analysis of the situation shows Hathaway where the problems lie. Because 60% of the companies that need the software know that it exists, advertising to build awareness is not necessarily the first priority. Next, a severe problem is revealed: Most prospects never have an opportunity to buy the product because only 20% have access to it. None of the programs Hathaway was considering will address this issue. She needs to consider new programs and approaches rather than simply choose from what others have brought to her.

Steps Four and Five yield encouraging numbers, but there is definitely room for improvement in both motivation and purchase. An addition to the sales force may be a good option, depending on what marketing research shows will influence customer behavior.

Step Six reveals another problem: Customers are not learning to use the product after they buy it. Investment in user-friendly features now looks like a very good option. While they are at it, the software engineers need to incorporate new core features that will raise the proportion of those who experience value above 50%.

Assume for a moment that Hathaway has unlimited money and adopts all these programs: an enlarged sales force, product quality improvements, and wider availability through several Internet distributors so that access rises substantially. Exhibit 1-4 shows how these interventions affect the outcome. After a lot of hard work, planning, and a substantial financial investment, Hathaway sees her loyal customers grow from 200 companies to more than 4000.

Of course, marketers rarely have an unlimited budget, and all programs do not have stellar results. In a more realistic world, Hathaway has finite marketing funds and faces serious time constraints. Assume that she can choose only one program, and it must be quick and relatively inexpensive to implement. Hathaway

EXHIBIT 1-4
Multiple CLC Interventions Affect Outcomes for Aries Software

Step in the CLC	Percentage Through Just This Step	Number of Companies Through Process Thus Far	Marketing Intervention	New Percentage Through Just This Step	Number of Companies Through Process Thus Far
⇓ Need	25%	100,000			100,000
⇓ Aware	60%	60,000	Advertising campaign	75%	75,000
⇓ Access	20%	12,000	New channels	60%	45,000
⇓ Motivate	50%	6000	Additional salespeople	70%	31,500
⇓ Purchase	40%	2400	Additional salespeople	60%	18,900
⇓ Know-how	33%	800	User-friendly features	75%	14,175
⇓ Experience value	50%	400	New core features	60%	8505
⇓ Retain	50%	200		50%	4253

determines that Aries could fairly easily increase distribution through Internet sellers, and access is clearly a weak spot in the company's relationship with its customers. Hathaway makes this change, and what happens is revealed in Exhibit 1-5. Because this change ripples through the rest of the customer decision-making process, Aries moves from 200 customers to 600, a 300% increase.

Choosing High-Return Programs

So far, our discussion has focused on marketing interventions that affect sales volume, but the CLC takes marketing insights one step farther. Let us return to Aries Software to see how each component of the CLC works.

Recall that Hathaway considered increasing the size of the sales force, which will cost $200,000, and making the software more user friendly, which will require a $300,000 investment. Which should she choose, if either? Which investment will pay off

EXHIBIT 1-5
One CLC Intervention Affects the Outcome for Aries Software

Step in the CLC	Percentage Through Just This Step	Number of Companies Through Process Thus Far	Marketing Intervention	New Percentage Through Just This Step	Number of Companies Through Process Thus Far
⇓ Need	25%	100,000			100,000
⇓ Aware	60%	60,000		60%	60,000
⇓ Access	20%	12,000	New channels	60%	36,000
⇓ Motivate	50%	6000		50%	18,000
⇓ Purchase	40%	2400		40%	7200
⇓ Know-how	33%	800		33%	2400
⇓ Experience value	50%	400		50%	1200
⇓ Retain	50%	200		50%	600

most handsomely? The CLC financial model can help Aries decide the best leverage point for its money based on a clear-cut analysis that will show how many more software packages will be sold under each option and the profit contribution of each. The model does this by building in another component: cost.

Hathaway can examine her original set of options and consider the incremental revenue per dollar of marketing expenditure each will produce. This is one way to decide, in a world of limited resources, which programs to fund out of the following array:

Run a new advertising campaign	$120,000
Add new channels of distribution	$200,000
Add two additional salespeople	$200,000
Add user-friendly features	$300,000
Add new core features	$500,000

When cost and revenue implications are incorporated, the new CLC in Exhibit 1-6 emerges. (Details of the computations appear in Appendix 1.)

Hathaway now has additional information to use in evaluating programs, both absolutely and relative to one another. One intervention does not even pay for itself: New core features will generate less than the cost to make the changes. The traditional business-to-business solution—add salespeople—generates the third lowest return, and a program not even considered initially— additional channels—produces the highest return by far. Clearly, the CLC model will help Hathaway eliminate some options, at least at their current cost level, and begin to choose among others.

The CLC analysis can be a springboard for thinking about your marketing situations in new ways, such as identifying new marketing programs that address several steps at once. For example, Hathaway could develop advertisements with information about how to use the software more effectively and commission market research to determine whether these advertisements increase not only awareness but also knowledge of how to use the product. As illustrated in Exhibit 1-7, if the latter increases only 17 points, from 33% to 50%, the revenue gain added to the gain in awareness ($612,500) yields a revenue-to-expense figure of $5.10. The educational advertisements become the second most attractive program. They cost $120,000, less than the $200,000 for additional salespeople, and may be a better fit for the Aries

EXHIBIT 1-6
Cost/Benefit Analysis of Aries Software Options

Step in the CLC	Percentage Through Just This Step	Number of Companies Through Process Thus Far	Marketing Intervention	New Percentage Through Just This Step	Additional Revenue from Just This Program[a]	Cost of program ($000)	Additional Revenue per Dollars of Expense
⇓ Need	25%	100,000					
⇓ Aware	60%	60,000	New advertisements	75%	$ 175	$120	$1.46
⇓ Access	20%	12,000	New channels	60%	$1,400	$200	$7.00
⇓ Motivated	50%	6000	Add salespeople	70%	$ 770	$200	$3.85
⇓ Purchase	40%	2400	Add salespeople	60%			
⇓ Know-how	33%	800	User-friendly features	75%	$ 875	$200	$4.38
⇓ Experience value	50%	400	New core features	60%	$ 140	$300	$ .47
⇓ Retain	50%	200		50%			

[a]Assumes that only one program changes at a time and that all other percentages remain as they were in the original CLC analysis (Exhibit 1-3).

budget. Advertising also may be a simpler alternative to hiring new people and reorganizing the sales force.

The CLC method equips you to build knowledge of the marketplace and base support program decisions on reliable numbers. Information about the costs and revenue contributions of different programs will lead to better choices as well as more accurate sales projections. The following are some questions to consider in making those evaluations:

EXHIBIT 1-7
Cost/Benefits Analysis of a Program That Affects Two Steps in the CLC

Step in the CLC	Percentage Through Just This Step	Number of Companies Through Process Thus Far	Marketing Intervention	New Percentage Through Just This Step	Additional Revenue from Just This Program	Cost of program ($000)	Additional Revenue per Dollars of Expense
⇓ Need	25%	100,000					
⇓ Aware	60%	60,000	*New advertisements	75%	$175K	$120K	$1.46
⇓ Access	20%	15,000					
⇓ Motivated	50%	7500					
⇓ Purchase	40%	3000					
⇓ Know-how	33%	1200	*Advertisements explain how to use	40%	$175	Same $120 as above	($175 + $175)/ 120 = $2.91
⇓ Experience value	50%	600					
⇓ Retain	60%	360					

360 × $3,500 = $1,260,000 − $700,000 = $560,000.

- How expensive is the new program, including such hidden costs as media placement, benefits and training for new employees, or additional corporate overhead as sales increase?
- Will increased sales be truly incremental or will they cannibalize other products, services, or divisions of the company?
- Will new sales levels be lasting or only a short-term response to a new program? Will long-term effects be as good as short-term effects?
- Would sales increase without this program? How can you determine what is causing an increase?
- Will it be difficult to return prices to their original level if new programs involve price reductions and special promotions?

■ How will the competition respond? How will that affect the success and cost of the program?
■ Will any of the programs cost more than the revenue they generate?

There also are questions that compare one program to another:

■ Which of these programs has or will have the greatest effect on sales?
■ Which programs have the greatest return per dollar of expenditure?

Advantages of the Customer Learning Curve

The CLC method offers marketers in particular and the whole company in general several specific benefits. First, the CLC identifies leverage points in both mature and new businesses. By examining decision making from the customer's point of view, you will discover where a product or service is succeeding and where the path is blocked. Consequently, you can concentrate money and energy where they will create the greatest incremental sales and profits.

Second, the CLC fosters integrated marketing. It demonstrates that a focus on one area—advertising, sales, training, and so forth—is not sufficient to take the customer all the way through the learning process. By examining the continuum of marketing plans and programs, you will arrive at an integrated and interdependent marketing approach. Furthermore, each aspect of this approach will be measurable, with well-defined objectives.

Third, the CLC focuses attention on the customer. Internal issues can cloud insight, but our method moves you past these distractions and keeps the strategic emphasis where it belongs: on attaining the full potential of the company's products and services.

Fourth, the CLC expands opportunities. Right from Step One—developing a new understanding of who needs a product or service—the emphasis is on broadening marketing perspectives to identify completely new targets.

Fifth, the CLC supports fact-based creativity. The more specific the marketing barrier is to overcome, the more creative and effective you can be.

Sixth, the CLC helps practitioners focus attention on improvement, not blame. Creativity and energy can be concentrated on what really counts, on building the customer base, sales, and profits, not on retrospective analysis of who or what went wrong.

A CHAPTER BY CHAPTER OVERVIEW

Here is how this book will help you understand and use the steps of the Customer Learning Curve.

Chapter 2: Who Needs What Your Company Sells?

Two opposite aspects of "target" are examined: the expansive, creative search for new prospects and procedures for counting and defining the target so programs can be implemented accurately. Also discussed are segmentation of business-to-business markets and positioning to capitalize on each segment's unique characteristics and variable needs.

Chapter 3: Who Is Aware of Your Offering and Its Benefits?

A deeper definition of "awareness" is presented, which encompasses knowledge of the benefits of your product or service as well as its existence. There are ideas on how to communicate benefits through the sales force, advertising, and other tools, including electronic media. This chapter also shows you how to adapt classic awareness-building tools to the business-to-business environment and addresses the perennial questions: How much advertising is enough? How do I choose among communication tools? and How do I measure awareness in a meaningful way?

Chapter 4: Who Can Access Your Product or Service?

The focus is on how customers who are aware of the benefits of your product or service can be blocked from ready access to it and what actions you can take. This chapter begins to explore the implications of e-commerce for business-to-business marketers: why old approaches are no longer adequate, current and future trends in e-commerce, and how to use e-commerce to build a competitive advantage for your company. It also identifies red flags that warn you when access changes need to be addressed and discusses ways to design new or amended channels.

Chapter 5: Are Your Customers Motivated?

There are ways to overcome the customer inertia that plagues so many business-to-business marketers. Key issues include determining who to motivate and how to excite a wide variety of potential purchasers—from administrative assistants to chief executive officers. The chapter describes the different uses for intrinsic and extrinsic motivators and how to identify demotivators that may be blocking purchase. It closes with information on how to determine the true cost of motivation programs, a key component to the mathematical analysis offered by the CLC model.

Chapter 6: What Influences Purchase? Pricing and Selling Your Product or Service

A vital aspect of purchase is price. This chapter discusses how to evaluate the effect of your prices on purchase, how to deal with competitive pricing activities, and how to manage pricing within your own company. It also examines the sales force from the perspective of the strategic marketer, the person responsible for integrating the efforts of sales and marketing in bringing about actual purchase. It includes a section on how e-commerce changes the role of the sales force and how it blurs the line between sales and marketing.

Chapter 7: Who Learns How to Use Your Product or Service?

You need to make sure that customers successfully learn to use the product or service they have purchased. This chapter provides fresh techniques for helping customers do that: reach into their organizations to discover barriers to effective usage and ways to customize learning programs, use segmentation to understand different customers and their learning needs, and deal with rapidly changing learning environments. We describe effective learning programs that serve as loyalty-builders in competitive environments.

Chapter 8: Do Your Customers Experience Value?

An area often overlooked by marketing is whether customers feel that the benefits they receive from a product or service are worth the price they paid. This chapter explores new techniques for measuring customer satisfaction and how to convert the insights gained into competitive advantage. Also discussed are internal integration efforts so that your company has a seamless program across different functional areas for generating customer satisfaction.

Chapter 9: Are You Creating Loyal Users?

The last step of the CLC is building loyalty that leads to customer retention. The first issue this chapter addresses is how to determine customer loyalty, including research approaches that track individual customers and their characteristics. Next, we discuss customers the marketer does *not* want to retain and why it is important to identify them. Finally, several fresh and effective loyalty-building programs are described.

Chapter 10: How to Create Profits from Marketing Chaos

The entire CLC approach is reviewed to show how both the mathematical and insight components interact. Also, we address the important question of how to lead an organization to adopt the CLC approach, including its use in decisions about resource allocation and marketing activities. Finally, we emphasize the role of the strategic marketer in the high-potential chaos of the twenty-first century.

Now, let's begin.

APPENDIX 1
Calculation of Incremental Revenue

	Need	Aware	Access	Motivate	Purchase	Know-How	Experience Value	Retain			Incremental Revenue
New Advertising Campaign											
Base	25%	60%	20%	50%	40%	33%	50%	50%			
	25%	15%	3%	1.5%	.60%	.20%	.10%	.05%			
	100,000	60,000	12,000	6000	2400	800	400	200	200	$ 700,000	
New Advertisements	25%	75%	20%	50%	40%	33%	50%	50%			
	25%	19%	3.75%	1.88%	.75%	.25%	.12%	.06%			
	100,000	75,000	15,000	7500	3000	1000	500	250	250	$ 875,000	$ 175,000
New Channels											
Base	25%	60%	20%	50%	40%	33%	50%	50%			
	25%	15%	3%	1.5%	.60%	.20%	.10%	.05%			
	100,000	60,000	12,000	6000	2400	800	400	200	200	$ 700,000	
New Channels	25%	60%	60%	50%	40%	33%	50%	50%			
	25%	15%	9%	4.5%	1.8%	.60%	.30%	.15%			
	100,000	60,000	36,000	18000	7200	2400	1200	600	600	$2,100,000	$1,400,000
Additional Salespeople											
Base	25%	60%	20%	50%	**40%**	33%	50%	50%			
	25%	15%	3%	1.5%	.60%	.20%	.10%	.05%			
	100,000	60,000	12,000	6000	2400	800	400	200	200	$ 700,000	
New Salespeople	25%	60%	**20%**	**70%**	**60%**	33%	50%	50%			
	25%	15%	3%	2.1%	1.26%	.42%	.21%	.10%			
	100,000	60,000	12,000	8400	5040	1680	840	420	420	$1,470,000	$ 770,000
User-Friendly Features											
Base	25%	60%	20%	50%	40%	**33%**	50%	50%			
	25%	15%	3%	1.5%	.60%	.20%	.10%	.05%			
	100,000	60,000	12,000	6000	2400	800	400	200	200	$ 700,000	
New Features	25%	60%	20%	50%	40%	**75%**	50%	50%			
	25%	15%	3%	1.5%	.60%	.45%	.23%	.11%			
	100,000	60,000	12,000	6000	2400	1800	900	450	450	$1,575,000	$ 875,000

APPENDIX 1
Continued

	Need	Aware	Access	Motivate	Purchase	Know-How	Experience Value	Retain	Incremental Revenue
New Core Features									
Base	25%	60%	20%	50%	40%	33%	50%	50%	
	25%	15%	3%	1.5%	.60%	20%	.10%	.05%	
	100,000	60,000	12,000	6000	2400	800	400	200	200
									$ 700,000
New Features	25%	60%	20%	50%	40%	33%	60%	50%	
	25%	15%	3%	1.5%	.60%	20%	.12%	.06%	
	100,000	60,000	12,000	6000	2400	800	480	240	240
									$ 840,000
									$ 140,000

Chapter 2

Who Needs What Your Company Sells?

The first step of the Customer Learning Curve is deceptively simple: Determine who needs your product or service, whether they know they need it or not. This step is important because the better a company can describe its target market, the more effective its marketing strategies and activities will be. Marketing funds will be invested where they generate the greatest return. The sales force will waste less time on nontargets. Communication messages will resonate with the prospect and shorten the sales cycle. A common set of customer expectations will be easier to meet and exceed.

How can you identify the perfect target market and walk the delicate line between defining need too narrowly and too broadly? The more narrowly defined the target market is, the sooner it will be mined out, saturated with competitors, and unable to produce the revenue growth demanded by corporate planners and ultimately by Wall Street. Sustained growth requires expansive, creative thinking. Powerful marketing strategies and efficient execution require focus. You must simultaneously expand and focus your creative market definition to reach your highest potential sales and profits.

It can be difficult to balance focus and expansion because, just as individuals feel more comfortable with one or the other of these complementary principles, whole companies can lean in one direction or the other. Furthermore, as business conditions change, a company may need to shift from focused to expansive thinking, or vice versa. Regardless of the particular challenge, the solution is the same: No longer can a company choose between expansion and focus. Rather, the successful company needs to pursue both simultaneously.

Thousands of years ago, Chinese sages created a metaphor for looking at the constant and puzzling paradoxes of the world around them. At any given moment, the world seemed out of balance, discordant; over the long run, however, the forces of life seemed to balance out. Drought was followed by flood; fire by ice; plenty by hunger. And then the adjustments would begin all over again.

The image that these philosophers developed is yin and yang, or two opposite principles that constantly shift yet continuously seek balance. Yang is the focused, the energetic. Yin is more fluid and softly expansive. Over time, they create a balance, a harmony of movement, but at any given moment the workings of yin and yang may seem confused, chaotic, and out of control.

For you, the user of the CLC, the yin of achieving balance is to create expansive ideas about who might, under a wide variety of circumstances, need and want a product or service. The yang is to take these ideas and organize, classify, and harness them into a focused strategy that is directed at a clearly identified, defined, and discrete group of potential users.

Creative yin alone never gets the job done. Disciplined yang alone drives the business into the ground. Pursued simultaneously, yin and yang, expansiveness and focus, sustain success.

YIN MARKET EXPLORATION: EXPANDING DEFINITIONS

To maximize the number of customers who qualify for Step One of the CLC, great business-to-business strategic marketers expand the definition of who needs their product or service. They courageously reject the cautious approach—defining the market to be as small as possible so it is easier to make impressive gains—and envision new possibilities.

This kind of vision is essential for a new technology or radically new product or service, because past experience is typically not directly predictive. But for mature products or services, it is just as important to look right through the boundaries of traditional market definitions. Marketers in both the new and the mature categories need to create a clear, innovative view of targets. The challenge for the new product or service is that it does not have a history. The challenge for the mature product or service is that it does.

In each case, you need a systematic way to explore possibilities, quantify their attractiveness, and defend the vision of the new from naysayers. You need to ask certain questions to catalyze creative exploration. Exhibit 2-1 diagrams how these questions lay out the expansive path for a mature product or service—from the

EXHIBIT 2-1
Yin Questions: Seeking New Markets for a Mature Product or Service

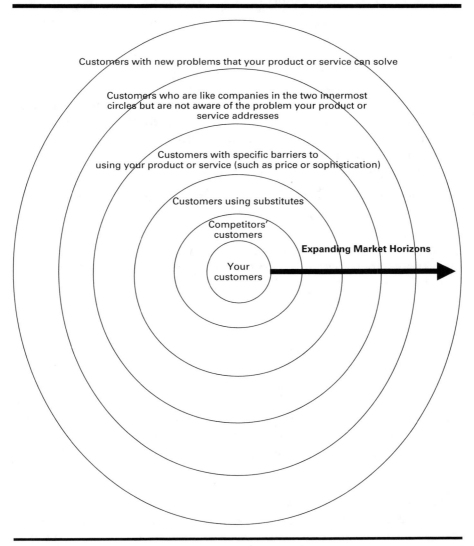

Customers with new problems that your product or service can solve

Customers who are like companies in the two innermost circles but are not aware of the problem your product or service addresses

Customers with specific barriers to using your product or service (such as price or sophistication)

Customers using substitutes

Competitors' customers

Your customers

Expanding Market Horizons

customers you know to the potential customers you are trying to understand. For mature products or services, the path to maximizing the customers who pass through the first step of the CLC begins with an understanding of who currently buys what you are selling and why. The marketer asks: Are there other people like the current customers who are not buying what I am selling? These include competitors' customers and prospects who are not yet buying from anyone. Another pair of questions expands the definition: Are there benefits of my product or service that current customers do not realize? Do these benefits open up new markets to pursue? A radically new product or service has no current customers and no direct competitors, so the questions are a little different. For example, rather than ask who currently buys your product, ask who purchases the technologies the new product or service will replace.

The CLC offers seven techniques to strategic marketers who want to develop new, powerful answers to the yin questions. These techniques are a guide to expansive thinking and have worked well for many companies, whether used to define targets for new products or to revitalize or reinvent mature ones.

Yin Technique One: Internal Ideation Sessions

Intuit regularly convenes its customer service representatives—the people in direct contact with customers—and asks them to generate ideas about new products, new applications, and new ways to reach and serve existing and new customers. 3M assembles cross-functional groups that include not only sales and service people but also bench technicians and even particularly creative and trustworthy customers. Chaparral Steel systematically convenes cross-functional teams for shared problem solving to practice the philosophy that progress is everyone's business.

Internal ideation sessions that focus on expanding the definition of who needs what the company sells start with people who have an intimate knowledge of the product or service. Participants are asked to let their thoughts flow freely about who might need that offering and how many different ways it might be used. The objective is to amplify thinking by drawing on the expertise and imagination of creative people.

You can foster the expansive thinking of this group in two ways. First, include divergent thinkers. Every organization has people who refuse to stick to the agenda because they always raise another aspect of an issue to consider. Often they are viewed as thorns in the side, and inviting them into the need phase of research is unlikely to yield peace and harmony. But that is not what you want in an ideation session, and divergent thinkers are almost certain to motivate the group to generate new ideas about customers and product or service usage.

Second, seek diverse perspectives. Traditionally, personnel from marketing, manufacturing, engineering, finance, and technical support take part in ideation sessions, but forward-looking companies now include a customer or two who can ask provocative, real-world questions. (More on this follows.) Often outsiders—academics, consultants, suppliers, and customers—add a unique twist to the group's thinking. A relatively new but successful member of the sales force or a junior product manager may have an interesting viewpoint, as may the chairman emeritus of the board of directors. The idea is not to generate chaos but to create a stew of ideas and approaches with many different flavors and textures.

Yin Technique Two: Involve Customers

L.L.Bean points with pride to the fact that when the company founder made his original product—the field boot—every one of the first 100 pairs came back with reported defects. Bean solved the problems and developed a superior product whose successors are still field tested today. Business-to-business companies follow a similar procedure when they have users beta test a piece of software or a new piece of equipment.

Why not "beta test" your ideation session's two or three best market definition ideas? Perhaps customers will catch the divergent thinking spirit and respond with suggestions about markets and applications your internal team never imagined. Or customers may modify your ideas in just the right way to make them work. Still others may point out problems that, when solved, will open significant new markets.

Yin Technique Three: Observe Customers Using What You Sell

Most customers are as bound to traditional definitions and parameters as are companies. Fresh, analytical observation of a product or service in use can uncover opportunities to change or augment it, or reveal ways the customer can alter processes to extract more value from the product or service offering.

In some cases experts, such as engineers, anthropologists, or market researchers, go into a customer's environment. They may discover not only mistakes and problems in using a product or service but also creative, unintended ways customers have found for the product or service to make a contribution. In other cases, customers are brought to a research facility and shown new ways to use a product or service. They are asked to replicate the demonstration, and observers note problems and mistakes as well as gather comments and suggestions.

In both these settings, the point of the observation is not just to fix problems. Whether the observer is you, a product or service expert, or a member of the ideation group who wants to refresh his or her thinking, the result can be ideas about new target markets and how best to approach them.

Yin Technique Four: Hire the Young

In their book *Blown to Bits,* Evans and Wurster (1999) point out that in industries in which physical products and information or relationships are bound together (as in publishing or financial services), the digital revolution creates discontinuities and radically different opportunities. The best way to understand what these opportunities mean for a given company may be to take advantage of what study after study reveals: the propensity of younger people to use technology with ease, as a natural part of their approach to problem solving. Young people can provide vivid insights into new possibilities of technology for almost any product or service, especially if you foster their ideas and approaches and include them in ideation sessions, product development, and marketing strategy planning.

Yin Technique Five: Dig Deeper into the Customer's Thinking

Customers are not always fully aware of their attitudes and beliefs about a product or service, their need for it, and how it can work for them. Furthermore, many customers do not find it easy to describe their deeper level of thinking and feeling. New research techniques can be used effectively to tap these customers and expand company thinking.

One of the most original methods, Zaltman Market Exploration Techniques (ZMET), is an amalgam of several powerful in-depth research tools. Created by Jerry Zaltman (see also

Zaltman and Barabba 1991), a professor of marketing at Harvard Business School, ZMET focuses on quality rather than quantity: A major research project may use only 15 or 20 subjects.

First, the research team meets with the client company to develop a highly specific yet open-ended focus for the research project. At this time, the target research population is also defined. Coca-Cola, for example, wanted to find out, at a much deeper level than traditional research could indicate, what its product meant to users and potential users.

Next, participants are chosen. They are given the research topic and asked to spend some time over the next two weeks collecting approximately a dozen visual images—from magazines and photos to their own art work—that somehow relate to their feelings and perceptions about that topic. They do not need to think about why they chose these images, but simply bring them to the interview. ZMET uses visual images because they bypass the censoring that often occurs in verbally oriented market research.

Each subject then spends two or three hours with a researcher, who uses a variety of indirect interviewing techniques to explore the subject's subconscious. Each interviewee then works with a computer videographer to create a video collage of the images chosen and an audio tape explanation of the collage.

Researchers code interview notes and tabulate them to identify themes related to the research topic. The audio tapes and videos are used in the final research report to enhance and broaden the client's understanding of the subjects' perspectives and feelings. ZMET works because it not only bypasses any verbal limitations of subjects but also encourages the client to see both need and motivation to buy from a fresh and expansive perspective. (For more information on ZMET, see the "Notes" section at the end of this chapter.)

Yin Technique Six: Restructure Focus Groups

Market research usually tries to pin down subjects, responses, and numbers. Even "soft" research such as focus groups often is designed to *limit* options. In contrast, yin, or expansive thinking, is about *increasing* options and broadening a tight focus.

Open-ended focus groups can contribute to expansive thinking. A good moderator delves into how participants think rather than run through a detailed set of questions. Participants can be chosen from a broader demographic or psychological set than is usually the case in order to get divergent views. The findings of these groups can freshen your thinking, especially about expansive ways to define the need for a product or service.

Yin Technique Seven: Research Intent to Buy

Research on purchase intention is traditionally used for concept tests and estimates of new product demand, so it often fits wells into Step One of the CLC. The product manager and the researcher write a brief statement that describes the features and benefits of a product. The researcher presents this to a potential customer and asks: "How likely is it that you would buy this product if it cost $X?" The amount is usually set at a realistic level but on the low side, to rule out borderline rejections because of price. The respondent chooses one answer from a range of options, such as "Definitely would purchase," "Might or might not purchase," and "Definitely would not purchase."

The yang approach to purchase intention research adds all the positive responses to half the "probables" and uses the sum as a rule-of-thumb estimate of demand. The yin approach goes on to ask: "Why did you answer as you did?" Probing the "probables" may reveal unanticipated reasons to buy that can expand the market. Understanding the negative responses gives the company specific direction about the problems to solve in order to access these potential customers. A large telecommunications company used intent-to-buy research in this way and broadened its definition of who needed one of its products in a business-to-business setting.

The company wanted to pin down potential small office/home office (SOHO) customers for its voice mail service. The responses to the intent to purchase question were as follows:

Definitely would buy	12%
Probably would buy	9%
Might or might not buy	12%
Probably would not buy	19% ⎫
Definitely would not buy	48% ⎬ 67%
	100

A traditional (yang) estimate of demand gave the company a target of 16.5%: all the definites (12%) and half the probables (4.5%). Of these, 8% already subscribed to voice mail, which reduced the potential new users to 8.5% of the marketplace. The company did not stop there. An investigation of why respondents answered as they did revealed the following about the group that probably or definitely would not buy (67%):

- 3% once had voice mail but disconnected because it was "too expensive." They did not say they did not need it; they said it was too expensive.
- 45% had a telephone answering machine. Again, they did not say they did not need voice messaging.
- 10% considered voice mail too expensive, similar to the former users.
- 6% reported they did not get enough calls to justify voice mail.
- 1% did not like machines.
- 2% stated they just did not need voice mail but gave no reason.

The marketing manager regarded each group of "whys" as a different segment and developed marketing plans tailored to overcome the groups' negative thinking (yin approach) rather than write these groups off (yang approach). For the two groups that considered voice mail too expensive, he developed a compelling list of additional benefits to justify the expense. For example, voice mail does not need to be turned off or on, so they will never miss a call. Voice mail can take a message rather than give callers a busy signal. Even one sale per month saved by voice mail can more than pay for the service. Rather than reduce the price of the service, he emphasized benefits and supported current pricing.

The largest potential group was the 45% that had an answering machine. These people must replace their machine when it breaks, so advertising emphasized that voice mail works 24 hours a day, 365 days a year, with no down time for repairs or replacement. Also, a "voice mail in a box" package was created for the electronics retailer's shelf, so when customers went to the store to replace a broken machine, they saw the network-based alternative.

Advertising targeted at those who did not get enough calls to justify voice mail (6%) emphasized that each call they did not receive was all the more important. They had better not miss even one call, and the only way to be sure was to subscribe to voice mail.

For those who did not like machines (1%), voice mail was positioned as the ideal solution—no equipment in your house, nothing to break, nothing to remember to turn on. A single question—why—provided not only the incentive to advertise and promote voice mail to the SOHO market but also specific ideas about how to present benefits, how to overcome objections, and how to motivate customers to buy. The company's subsequent success in penetrating this market clearly shows the importance of looking beyond traditional market definitions to determine who can receive value from a product.

YANG MARKET ANALYSIS AND SEGMENTATION IN STEP ONE OF THE CLC

Yang or "focused" market analysis organizes facts and harnesses information to quantify need. The key question is: "How large is the potential market?" It also segments the market, identifying distinct groups of potential users who warrant different marketing strategies. Because it quantifies, yang research serves as the basis for financial projections and for the evaluation of various ways to increase sales, which are vital parts of the CLC. Because it describes segments, yang research guides sales force targeting, time allocation, and message definition.

Yang analysis techniques include internally generated information on sales by volume and dollar, production costs, and sales force performance; market surveys that track customer satisfaction and buying behavior; statistical information available from the government, trade associations, and industry monitoring groups; and feedback from customer contact employees (sales and customer service representatives).

Yang research is most powerful when it finds a way to use the numbers to corroborate the creative insights of yin exploration, especially yin notions about how to segment the market and look at customers in ways that generate competitive advantage. The goal of yang research is to develop a clear definition and multidimensional picture of each newly envisioned target group. This enables the company to target marketing efforts more effectively and efficiently than competitors that are laboring under traditional market definitions.

All too often, marketers fall back on firmographics—the corporate equivalent of demographics, such as the size, industry, and geographical market of a firm—in defining target groups. This is particularly tempting in business-to-business marketing, because the sales force wants unmistakable and easily understood criteria. But such easy markers as size or industry code miss valuable marketing opportunities because companies within each industry and size group differ substantially. These differences may stem from operational aspects, such as how the customer applies or uses your product or service; preferred buying channels; or buying procedures (committee or individuals, request for proposal or closed bid, and so on). Other differences may be due to company philosophy and identity, such as risk profile (innovators or slow adopters of new ideas). Still others may relate to the benefits different companies seek from the same product or service or to unique adaptations they want and need. Each of these characteristics creates segments you can target and serve differently and more accurately than your competitors.

Some specific techniques can be used to identify and target segments of your market. This kind of segmentation lays the groundwork for improving your ability to determine who needs your product, which enhances your performance on the first step of the CLC.

Yang Segmenting Secret One: Identify Who Not to Visit

The Wholesale Industry Practice Area of a large professional service firm wanted to increase its client base. Research indicated that more technologically savvy wholesalers were the most likely customers. Using industry codes, the company identified more than 10,000 wholesalers in its geographic service area. How could the company determine which of these were technologically sophisticated and which, because of traditional relationships and methods, were not worth the trouble?

First, publicly available yang or "hard" information was used to rule out many potential targets and reduce the potential targets to 500 or fewer in each of several major metropolitan markets. For example, smaller companies were eliminated because they could not afford the sophisticated services the firm was selling.

Second, three yang research questions were asked: Do you calculate profit per customer? Do you do strategic planning? and Do you have a strategic plan for using information? The answers determined each company's attitude toward innovation. These questions could be answered by a telephone interview of lower level managers, who tend to be easily accessible. By focusing only on the companies that answered all three questions affirmatively, the firm further reduced the number of targets to 100 or 150 per major metropolitan area.

Third, five cities were selected for an initial rollout of the program; in each, four partner-manager teams contacted 25–35 targets per team. Almost half the companies contacted agreed to visits, and almost half of these eventually became clients. For every 100 of the initial contacts, more than 20 projects per office were sold. This was more than ten times the usual success rate when the firm used an untargeted, firmographic approach.

This example illustrates several yang approaches to developing business-to-business segments and targets that lead directly to greater revenue and more efficient use of marketing resources. Arguably the single most valuable contribution of segmentation was the identification of 9700 wholesalers to ignore. Does this mean there were no prospects among them? No. But sending out partner-manager teams—a very expensive direct sales force—is the wrong way to approach such a large number of potential clients. To reach this group, a much more efficient and cost-effective method would be media campaigns and promotions to get these prospects to identify themselves. For example:

- Pull in people through the firm's Web site.
- Send e-mail to identified individuals in these companies asking if they want more information.
- Participate in trade shows for wholesalers.
- Advertise in specialty trade journals.
- Conduct seminars for wholesalers.
- Commission broad-reach surveys (which would both bring the firm to top-of-mind awareness and identify interested customers).
- Send relevant books or articles or appropriate direct mail premiums along with an explanation of the firm's offerings.

By creating an "objective" tool for qualifying leads, the company sent the most expensive and most effective direct sales force to the best prospects—a group that could be expanded later.

Yang Segmenting Secret Two: Start with Firmographics but Add Product-Specific Criteria

Use firmographics to identify a set of customers, but refine targets on the basis of attitude, application, or benefits sought. As described above, the professional services firm sorted first on size and geography and then screened prospects according to their attitude toward technology. Several sorting approaches combine firmographics with experiences, attitudes, and values within companies to create richer and more provocative segment definitions while also taking account of sales force orientation. Seven methods are noted, as follows.

Acknowledge Geography

The sales force is almost always organized geographically. Even if geography is irrelevant to how customers buy and use your product or service, you probably need to map segments onto territories to set sales goals, allocate budgets, and guide sales force efforts. Occasionally, other aspects of your strategy should vary by geographic area. For example, it is illegal to charge interest in some Islamic countries, and sweepstakes are illegal in some states.

Consider Industry/Standard Industrial Classification Code

In regulated or recently deregulated sectors, such as utilities, telecommunications, and banking, industry definitely matters. Even in these sectors, however, there is typically as much variation within as between industries. At the very least, you should probably restate your general product position in industry-specific language.

Think About Customer Size

Sales personnel usually are organized according to the size of customers, and dozens or even hundreds may be assigned to serving the largest. Even if small companies buy and use your product in the same ways and for the same reasons as large companies, their smaller purchases do not justify expensive marketing programs. The Web is one way to serve these companies, with its technology-based service models, reliance on self-service, and low transaction costs.

Look at the Customer's Place in the Product Life Cycle

Customers' needs and desires may vary dramatically depending on the life cycle stage of their product, service, or industry. In the growth stage, companies may have such rapidly changing agendas that they are willing, for example, to pay a premium for extra services. Mature companies may be willing to invest in your product or service to gain even a small cost advantage over their competitors.

Consider Customer "Style" and Attitudes Toward Innovation

Some businesses want to keep doing things the same way; others think they can stay competitive only by embracing the new as quickly as possible. Each group can be a target but will require radically different positioning for your product or service. This is one segmentation factor that is taken into account by the professional service firm in the preceding example.

Understand How Customers Make Purchases

A company that uses only competitive bidding should not be approached the same way as a company whose interpersonal relationships play a key role in decision making. Knowledge about how companies buy is important in positioning your offering to them.

Know Whether Targets Buy from Competitors

Find out which competitor serves your targets. Different competitors tend to emphasize different benefits, and these can give marketers a valuable clue about what a company values in making purchases. Exhibit 2-2 illustrates how United Parcel Service (UPS) used a nested approach to segmentation, which combines customer characteristics with the power of application, attitude, and benefit segmentation. Firmographics identified targets, and deeper insight into management style helped predict receptivity to specific marketing strategies.

Here is how the procedure might work. In Segment 1 (size) are all companies with total annual sales of more than $1 billion. In Segment 2 (product) are the billion-dollar companies that also use Next Day Air^{SM}. In Segment 3 (industry) the companies are further narrowed to those in the direct mail retail business. In Segment 4 (role of product) the qualifying companies are refined to those that consider air service a normal way of doing business. This final group is the ultimate target.

In summary, how can you meet your need for rich segmentation definitions, using such sorting criteria and systems as those above, and still provide the sales force with target descriptions that make sense to them? The solution is to segment the market for your product strategically and then map these strategic segments onto the sales force's firmographic segments. This approach not only gives the sales force guidance on how to find the companies that need your product but also provides definitions to use as the basis for planning market strategies and programs.

EXHIBIT 2-2
Nested Segmentation UPS Used to Focus Marketing Efforts

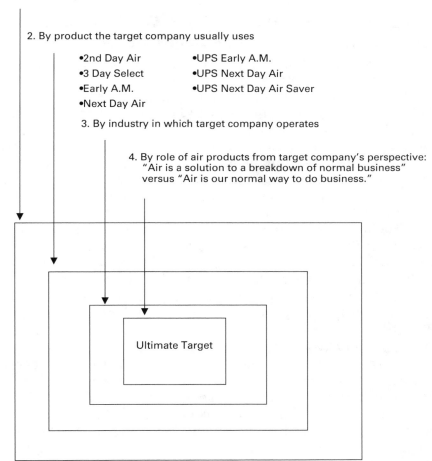

1. By size of the target company

  2. By product the target company usually uses

      •2nd Day Air   •UPS Early A.M.

      •3 Day Select   •UPS Next Day Air

      •Early A.M.   •UPS Next Day Air Saver

      •Next Day Air

    3. By industry in which target company operates

      4. By role of air products from target company's perspective:
         "Air is a solution to a breakdown of normal business"
         versus "Air is our normal way to do business."

Ultimate Target

Yang Segmenting Secret Three: Nail the Numbers

A critical step in setting marketing strategy is to estimate the number of potential customers and the potential revenue in each segment. A segment must be large enough to justify the expenditures required to target it, so accuracy is essential. Identifying too many or too few targets can be a major problem. An overestimate leads to unrealistic sales projections. An underestimate can be just as bad: If marketing programs are successful, the company may run out of stock or be unable to deliver services, which will alienate customers in the long run.

Yang Segmenting Secret Four: Go Beyond Rigid Definitions to Situational Segmentation

There is something almost irresistible about the idea that segments should be mutually exclusive. But to assign any given customer to one and only one segment is bad marketing. A customer could be in more than one segment at different times or in different segments at the same time. One person can have two distinct needs, which makes him or her a prime target for two different marketing mixes simultaneously. Leverage comes from defining the situations that create need and then targeting prospects in those situations, not from sorting prospects into mutually exclusive categories at all costs.

The mail room of a major corporation or professional service firm illustrates situational segmentation. On any given day, some outgoing packages are tagged for special pick-up and delivery by 8:30 A.M. the next day. The decision maker who selected this premium delivery service did so to solve a problem or take advantage of a time-sensitive opportunity; cost was relatively unimportant. But the same mail room contains letters and packages that are going to be delivered by second-day express and others that will go by first-class mail. The decision makers in these cases (perhaps the same people who chose the premium service) have judged that they can save a little money by accepting a later delivery time.

Should this company be included in the "price-insensitive" segment? The answer is yes. Should it be excluded from that segment? Again, yes. Clearly, it is the situation and not industry or size of the company that determines which service-price combination will be chosen.

Yang Segmenting Secret Five: Create a Different Marketing Mix for Each Segment

If you do not have a varied marketing mix, you do not have various segments. Segmentation should not be a sterile, intellectual exercise. Rather, it is a way to gain marketing leverage—both advantage and efficiency. Gaining leverage requires using different strategies for different prospects, or different strokes for different folks. The market for marketing consulting services provides a perfect illustration.

Frank Lynn & Associates, a Chicago-based marketing consulting firm, wanted to focus its practice development efforts as well as its service delivery processes. A survey of clients revealed two very different groups: innovators and mainstreamers. Innovators wanted state-of-the-art thinking, and mainstreamers wanted their problem solved. The company tailored its marketing mix to address the needs of each segment. Exhibit 2-3 shows the characteristics of these segments and how Frank Lynn & Associates used this information in its marketing mix.

Yang Segmenting Secret Six: Know Your Limits

Most products or services can target two or at most three segments. Cluster analysis that yields 23 groups may be statistically correct, but the organization that can cater to so many targets has yet to be formed. If the number of targets exceeds three, consider subdivision into new products or a new set of segment teams—and look for new channels so that traditional channels are not overloaded. If you identify five attractive segments with significantly different needs, then create different products for each segment. This can greatly expand your potential targets and avoid the confusion of offering exactly the same product or service to different target groups.

In the consumer marketing arena, Procter & Gamble has long been the leader in taking this tack. Is there truly a profound difference between one laundry soap and another? Usually the answer is no. But if product characteristics, packaging, advertising, and "identity" are finely tuned, products that are basically the same come to occupy quite different niches in the minds of consumers.

Yang Segmenting Secret Seven: Each Segment Has Its Own Customer Learning Curve

Each target segment must be approached with a completely different marketing strategy. An investment in building awareness may be just the thing for Segment A but virtually a waste of funds for Segment B. Strategic marketing calls for different approaches for each segment, but the only way to learn which leverage points

EXHIBIT 2-3
Segmentation for Marketing Consulting Services

A. Segment Characteristics

Attribute	Importance to Innovators	Importance to Mainstreamers
State-of-the-art thinking	Very high	Very low ("Want to stay away from the bleeding edge.")
Teach my people the latest techniques	Very high	Very low ("It would take away time from getting the job done.")
Solve my business problem	Very low ("That's my job. Give me the ideas and I'll solve the problem.")	Very high ("Just tell me what to do.")
Help with implementation	Very low ("We hire the best people. They can make it happen.")	Very high ("I need all the help I can get.")
Project timing	As fast as possible	Keep to schedule
Cost	Keep me informed of cost options	Stay on budget
Keep me informed	Very high	Very high
Quality of people on the consulting team	Very high	Very high

B. Marketing-Mix Implications

Element	Marketing Mix for Innovators	Marketing Mix for Mainstreamers
Product	Budget allocated to sophisticated analysis	Budget allocated to communicating solution to client
Promotion	Articles, speeches, thought-stimulating direct mail	Seminars on applications
Place	Direct selling by thought leaders	References from other mainstreamers
Price	Frequent communication of cost options	Sell "value"; manage to budget

are the same and which are different across segments is to calibrate a curve for each and compare them.

Yang Segmenting Secret Eight: Update and Innovate Regularly

Today's high leverage opportunity is tomorrow's mature market. When all fire trucks were made out of steel, Emergency One introduced the first lightweight, rust-resistant aluminum trucks and carved out a segment of fire departments that were innovative and preferred superior performance and economics to tradition. As the attractiveness of aluminum became apparent to other fire departments, competitors began offering similar products.

Emergency One responded by designing the next innovation: passenger areas that keep fire fighters safe and let them ride in a quieter cab, so they could plan their strategy on the way to a fire. Today, the company puts computers on board, which enables departments to track response time and provides the location of hydrants and hazardous materials. Although some fire departments are just plain innovative, each new concept from Emergency One slices the market a little differently and appeals to a different target.

Segmentation, especially when based on superior products or applications, does not last forever. It needs to be updated and replaced by new and more effective ways to divide your market.

THE STRATEGIC MARKETER'S RESPONSIBILITIES IN DEFINING NEED

Who should be responsible for bringing together and synthesizing these disparate and sometimes conflicting yin and yang explorations? Here is where the strategic marketer plays a key role. Regardless of the title—product manager, vice president of marketing, sometimes president or chief executive officer—several aspects of the strategic marketer's character are noteworthy. This person has wisdom, an ability to learn from both the flow of yin research and the discipline of the yang, and a fearless willingness to take responsibility for the company's future successes and failures. The strategic marketer can engage passionately or assess objectively, can lead or subtly guide. In the world of understanding customers, the strategic marketer is most likely a gifted, entrepreneurial thinker.

In the definition of need stage, the strategic marketer has three key tasks. Task 1 is to balance yin exploration and yang focus. Not only do you need to work with these two different approaches and often two different constituencies within a company, but you must also prod the organization never to rest on its laurels, regardless of successful marketing efforts in the past. You must keep the organization moving, redefining the market and renewing your company's strategies (yin). At the same time, you must focus the organization on continuously improving marketing execution (yang).

Task 2 is to develop segments that yield leverage. Any market can be segmented in a vast number of ways. Market research makes the problem worse when it generates file drawer after file drawer of uninterpreted facts. You must have the entrepreneurial vision to convert these facts into specific segment definitions and target market choices that yield marketing leverage.

Task 3 is to convince the organization to choose the best targets. If an organization can implement only three marketing mixes, you must convince top management to choose the three that are best for the company. This role is part analysis, part judgment, part communication, part credibility, and part character.

SUMMARY OF STEP ONE: DETERMINING NEED

Here are the key points to remember in determining who needs your product or service. First, determining need is a function of both expansive (yin) and focused (yang) thinking and research. Both are necessary, but they must be balanced and integrated for a company to remain dynamic and competitive.

Second, yin thinking involves several techniques and approaches that expand ideas about who needs a product or service in a wide variety of circumstances. Among these are ideation sessions, customer feedback, observation, the integration of young people and forward thinking into your company, and the use of new types of market research or old types in new ways. All can contribute to expansive thinking.

Third, yang approaches are used in many business-to-business companies already. Focus sales efforts on the best prospects, refine segment definitions and include situational segmentation, tighten up customer and revenue projections, customize the marketing mix, reduce the number of segments to target, create a unique CLC for each segment, and stay current on the market. All are useful ways to focus thinking.

Any approach to determining need is useful only when you, the strategic marketer, take responsibility for synthesizing findings, pinning down numbers, and making sure the company acts promptly and appropriately on its research findings.

Notes

For more information on ZMET and a current reference for Jerry Zaltman, see the Harvard Business School Web site (http://www.hbs.edu). At Zaltman's home page, click on "Research" or "Publications" for more information. The link Faculty/Marketing will also provide a link to "Mind of the Marketing Laboratory," which describes the research laboratory at Harvard Business School designed for ZMET work. The article, "Seeing the Voice of the Consumer: Metaphor-based Advertising Research," in the *Journal of Advertising Research* (35:4, July/August 1995, pp. 35–51) presents a detailed description of ZMET, including samples of the output of ZMET research. The article also includes a rich bibliography of related information. The most recent articles on ZMET are "Consumer Researchers: Take a Hike!" in the *Journal of Consumer Research* (26:4, March 2000, pp. 423–28) and "The ZMET Alternative" in *Marketing Research* (12, Summer 2000, pp. 6–12) by Gwendolyn Catchings-Castello.

Another interesting approach to depth market research is describe by G. Clotaire Rapaille in his book, *Seven Secrets of Marketing in a Multi-Cultural World* (Executive Excellence Publishing, 2001). Rapaille is a cultural anthropologist who has translated his work into a search for "archetypes" that influence customer thinking and behavior. His company, for example, conducted research that helped produce Chrysler's PT Cruiser.

For more information about fresh approaches to market research, see *Observational Research Handbook: Understanding How Customers Live with Your Product* by Bill Abrams (American Marketing Association/McGraw Hill, 2000).

Chapter 3

Who Is Aware of Your Offering and Its Benefits?

To measure market awareness of its next-day delivery service, UPS surveyed target businesses. More than 90% were aware of the service, but almost half could not give a specific reason they should use UPS rather than Federal Express or Airborne. Would it be accurate to say that awareness level was 90%? From the Customer Learning Curve perspective, the answer is a clear no. Why? Because the knowledge that something exists is not enough to move the prospect down the path to motivation and purchase. Prospects must know why they should buy the product or service instead of that offered by the competition—or instead of not purchasing at all—before the awareness job is finished.

A strong and dynamic direct sales force is a vital component of almost every business-to-business company's approach to building awareness, especially in highly technical situations or for sales that involve large amounts. Salespeople also can be essential in moving the customer through the later stages of the CLC. But the sales force cannot carry the whole burden of building awareness of benefits, motivating buyers, closing the sale, teaching customers how to use a product or service, guaranteeing satisfaction, and managing an ongoing relationship. That would be an inefficient use of an expensive resource at best or, at worst, an impossible task.

Many companies have greatly increased sales force productivity by adding awareness-building tools to support sales. Here are three examples:

■ BellSouth almost abandoned its Disaster Recovery suite of products and services when the sales force was unable to meet the launch plan's sales targets. When the advertising campaign added television news interviews during hurricane season and targeted print advertisements, sales soared. Salespeople had easier access to target customers who were interested in improving their disaster preparedness and were aware that BellSouth could help.

■ R.W. Beck, a prestigious engineering consulting firm, considered canceling participation in an annual trade show for municipalities because it did not build enough awareness to generate good sales leads. Instead, the company added several media events at the show, including a daily newsbriefing based on an issues survey administered in the company's booth and a drawing for a Hartman briefcase. To enter the drawing, prospects needed to complete the issues survey, which also asked if they would like a sales call from the company. Winners were announced on the closed-circuit television, and more people came to the booth. The convention generated more than 200 new contacts, all of whom were now aware of the kinds of benefits Beck's services could offer.

■ Accenture pioneered advertising of professional services to open doors, legitimize partners, and position the firm as distinct, differentiated professionals. Subsequently, expensive and time-consuming sales calls by partners resulted in much higher close rates than in the past.

Strategic marketers must decide how to use various awareness-building tools. They also must forge interfaces among functional areas—advertising, public relations, sales, e-commerce—to create integrated programs like those of BellSouth, R.W. Beck, and Accenture.

EACH MEMBER OF THE AWARENESS CAST HAS A ROLE

Advertising, public relations, direct mail, telemarketing, personal selling, and electronic communication all have a distinct part to play. The sales force is the traditional workhorse. Direct mail and telemarketing are popular among business-to-business marketers because they are familiar and their results are measurable. Web marketing is gaining popularity because it is cutting edge and can be inexpensive. In contrast, advertising and public relations may be underused because they are mysterious to the business-to-business mind.

Do not eliminate any of these tools from your resource base. In this communications-congested world, you need to get as many of your messages through to your prospects as possible. The rule of thumb in consumer advertising is that three impressions are required to transmit the message, and five are needed for complex products. Because business-to-business products tend to be complex or uniquely positioned, five is probably the number necessary. Buyers in the business-to-business world are just like any other consumers. They watch television, they listen to the radio during their commute, they scan the sports or entertainment pages. Although a personal sales call certainly makes a stronger impression than a billboard or radio advertisement, multiple impressions are almost always needed, and some cost significantly less than personal visits.

The issue is not whether to use multiple tools to build awareness but when to use them. Exhibit 3-1 compares six tools on two

EXHIBIT 3-1
Cost Per Impression and Flexibility of Awareness-Building Tools

Place each of these six tools on the following graph:

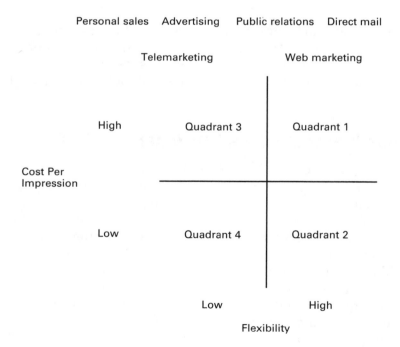

key dimensions: the flexibility of the message, or the extent to which it can be customized for each target buyer, and the cost per impression. Take a moment to consider where you would locate each of the six.

Personal sales fit best in Quadrant 1. Flexibility is high, because you can change the message for every prospect, but so is cost per sales call. Public relations goes into Quadrant 4 because it is difficult to customize but is virtually free. Direct mail falls in Quadrant 4 near the origin, telemarketing in Quadrant 1 near the origin.

With these relationships in mind, it appears that advertising and electronic marketing could be good choices for business-to-business companies.

ADVERTISING: A SURPRISE PLAYER

Most business-to-business marketers do not realize that advertising may be one of the lowest cost-per-impression tools. If the people who need a business-to-business product—the very people who must become aware of its benefits—number in the hundreds of thousands or more, mass market advertising is probably the least costly way to get the job done. A lively, engaging television advertisement can show a potential customer the benefits of a product on a multitude of levels, ranging from the intellectual to the deeply psychological.

The basic investment can be a barrier. For example, a page in *USA Today* costs more than $100,000, and a 30-second spot during Monday Night Football goes for $350,000. Furthermore, a sustained effect on potential buyers requires multiple advertisements at additional cost. Nevertheless, a large company with hundreds of thousands of prospects may find that such advertising is the most efficient part of its marketing mix. A small company may need to select advertising impressions a little more carefully: newsletters with real news delivered through regular mail or e-mail, advertisements in the trade journals your prospects read, trade-show booths with intriguing content, and fringe or spot television time.

Web Marketing: Still a Wild Card

Electronic marketing covers a cluster of different approaches, all of which are delivered through electronic communication. E-mails to potential customers are both highly flexible and inexpensive, after the investment is made in creating a strong address list.

A banner advertisement on someone else's Web site is not costly, but it is only efficient if the audience matches your particular target market. If just 1% of viewers correspond to those you want to reach, cost per impression with target buyers becomes more expensive.

A highly interactive Web site can achieve a high degree of flexibility. Each user can be offered a different set of products, a different benefit message, and even a different price. The development cost is high, but if millions of people visit your site, the cost per impression is low. This awareness-building method is efficient in reaching your targets only if you have a focused, multitool strategy for drawing the right people to the site.

The various awareness-building activities through electronic marketing end up at different points on our graph, as shown in Exhibit 3-2. Banner advertisements are in Quadrant 4, e-mail in Quadrant 2. A high-tech Web site could begin in Quadrant 1, become more efficient, and move toward Quadrant 4.

Evaluating and Choosing Among Options

Step Two of the CLC involves building awareness of your product or service. The addition of electronic tools to a mix that

EXHIBIT 3-2
Your Awareness-Building Tool Kit

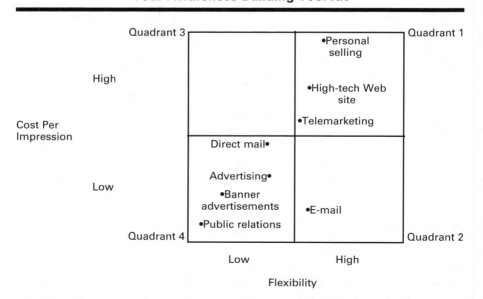

already includes advertising, direct marketing, a sales force, public relations, and educational approaches such as trade-show exhibits can quickly overwhelm you. Should your choices be based primarily on cost per impression? Flexibility? Total reach? Budget limitations? Finding the answer is more straightforward than you might think. Only three interacting factors need to be considered. First, who are you trying to reach? Second, what medium best lends itself to communicating the benefits you want to emphasize to your potential customers? Third, what is the most cost-effective way to capitalize on your answers to the first two questions?

Who needs your product or service builds on your findings in Step One of the CLC. What kind of person or company is the target? How do they like to be approached? What excites them, motivates them? How do they make decisions? If your product is display racks and shelving, the same selling approach cannot be used for discount stores and a regional chain of high-end clothing boutiques.

How to communicate your benefits requires some fresh thinking. If your business is creating state-of-the-art Web sites for *Fortune*-1000 companies, your medium of choice must be visual: your own Web site, obviously, but perhaps also television commercials that convey the kind of excitement you can bring to the Web. If you are selling a highly sophisticated lubricant for industrial equipment that capitalizes on a fresh approach to manipulating chemical structure, television advertising clearly is not the way to go. Aside from your own Web site, you might choose a public relations campaign that generates coverage in technical journals, advertisements in those journals, and presentations at trade shows for industrial chemists.

In selecting media, you may want to consider unusual or previously disregarded techniques. BellSouth, for example, wanted to increase sales of its technologically sophisticated frame relay product. Traditionally, a direct sales force had called on target customers, but this method was expensive, even when targets were carefully screened. The marketing team decided to explore a new way to increase awareness among medium and small companies: telemarketing. Conventional wisdom said this would never work: The product technology was too complex, telemarketing staff tends to be unsophisticated, and customers expect to be approached in person. The marketers designed a program that took these objections into account. Telemarketers were recruited differently, with an emphasis on technologically sophisticated and better-educated workers. A detailed training program was developed, as was a different compensation system. Not only was this sales effort successful, but the telemarketers also were an excellent recruiting pool for the field sales force. Putting a new spin on an old approach may work well, especially when done from a broader perspective.

Consider your budget and the cost per impression only after you determine who to reach and the best way to do that. There is always a way to manage awareness-building costs, when you know what you want and why you want it. Even the use of a direct sales force can be fine-tuned: The Web design company might send salespeople only after qualified leads are identified through the Web site, and the lubricant manufacturer may find it cost-effective to visit decision makers at all its major potential clients, to reinforce in person the technical breakthrough the product represents.

Exhibit 3-3 summarizes major awareness-building tools in terms of advantages, disadvantages, cost per impression, and effectiveness. This exhibit, combined with Exhibits 3-1 and 3-2, can be helpful in deciding which tools you should consider for your particular situation.

DOES BRANDING MATTER IN THE BUSINESS-TO-BUSINESS CUSTOMER LEARNING CURVE?

The short answer is yes. For example, Accenture commands premium prices in a highly competitive professional services market because of branding. McKinsey & Company, SAP, Bain, Intel, General Electric, Hale Pumps, and Cummins Engines are just a few of the many business-to-business companies that also command brand premiums.

From the CLC perspective, a strong brand is a learning shortcut because the product and its associated benefits are known to the prospect. Brand identity refers to what a product means to the prospect, to its position in the prospect's thoughts. At best, a brand represents reliability, quality, consistency, and an on-going "relationship," so the customer does not need to think very hard and long about purchase or repurchase.

Your awareness-building strategy is affected by brand strength. Take full advantage of a strong brand, and be sure that

EXHIBIT 3-3

A Comparison of Awareness-Building Tools

Tool	Pros	Cons	Cost Per Impression*	Measurability
Direct sales	Excellent for complex message Highly persuasive Highly flexible in answering questions Totally customized Creates partnerships	Expensive Requires well-trained sales force	Very high	Very good
Advertising	"Dramatic" potential Can be very persuasive Can be relatively inexpensive for large audiences	Often reaches many nontargets Long lead time Requires multiple exposures	Low	Requires market research
Direct mail	Can be customized to target Relatively fast turnaround Can provide a lot of information	Can get lost in the clutter	Moderate	Very good
Telemarketing	Can be customized to target Very fast turnaround Wider applications are possible	Can meet customer resistance	Moderate	Very good
Electronic	Can be customized to target Can have high education value Can supplement all other elements	Not familiar to some customers Can have high start-up costs	Low	Mixed
Public relations	Highly credible Can provide highly technical information	Can be hard to manage Usually cannot stand alone	Very low	Not good
Education	Can be customized to target Can be face-to-face Can provide highly technical information Creates partnership with target	Demands participation by target Can be expensive Usually long lead times	Moderate to high	Mixed

*Within target audience.

your message does not conflict with what customers already think about your brand. You can even extend brand identity, up to a point. Before recent events destroyed brand equity and financial health at WorldCom, the marketing team extended this brand name for long-distance services to complex data services for business-to-business customers. When WorldCom acquired UUNET, which had a preeminent reputation for strong Internet services, the marketers astutely retained the distinct brand. As the industry matured and the WorldCom brand continued to strengthen, the company de-emphasized UUNET, describing it as "a WorldCom Company," and eventually replaced the brand entirely.[1] Now that the company has been embroiled in controversy, it has wisely replaced the brand with "MCI," extending the old consumer brand to the full range of WorldCom products.

When a new offering does not fit easily into an existing brand, you can change your brand's image. This is expensive but may be necessary. Or it may be time to create a new brand to flank the old one or acquire an existing brand to serve the same purpose.

If your brand is not well known, you must intelligently build its position in the minds of prospects. The more crowded the brand category is, the more important it is to find a position that differs from that of competitors in an important way to your prospects.

As part of the strategy to differentiate your brand from others, formulate a positioning statement, which succinctly and clearly states the brand position you want to achieve. It should guide all the points of contact—advertising, promotions, sales, service, even packaging and billing—that prospects have with your brand. Exhibit 3-4 offers some suggestions for brand positioning. (For other sources on in-depth branding and positioning, see the "Notes" section at the end of this chapter.)

CLASSIC GUIDES FOR AWARENESS-BUILDING CAMPAIGNS

Several internal activities are extremely useful in planning awareness-building programs. These are typically performed by

---

[1]Market research, including an in-depth approach such as ZMET (Zaltman and Barabba 1991), can determine what your brand means and whether customers will extend those perceived qualities to a new product, service, or message.

EXHIBIT 3-4
Options for Brand Positioning

1. By product difference: a real or perceived advantage that is valuable to the target.
   Intel: Intel Inside

2. By key benefit or feature: an aspect that is valued by the target.
   Ernst & Young: There isn't a business we can't improve
   SAP: A better return on information

3. By special relationship with users: The product is designed especially for a particular target market.
   Microsoft: Where do you want to go today?
   Sprint: We help your business do more business
   AT&T: It's all within your reach

4. By usage occasion: how, when, or where the product is used.
   FedEx: When it absolutely, positively has to be there overnight.

5. By category: The product is its own category, so its value becomes greater than that of one special feature or benefit. Good with multiple products.
   Xerox: The Document Company
   Kinko's: Your Branch Office

6. By competitive advantage: feature or value greater than competitive offerings.
   Deloitte & Touche: Which Big Six firm will spend the next year focusing on your problems, not theirs?

7. By association: with an emotion, value, person, or lifestyle that the target desires, values, and perceives as positive.
   Corporate sponsorship of the Olympics

8. By solution to a problem: solves a problem common to the target.
   Ricoh: Simple solutions. Based on human needs.

product managers or those with day-to-day responsibility for products or services. Your role as strategic marketer is to review how these are done, ensure consistency, and determine whether they are fully supported by research findings and previous experience with the product.

Formulate a Positioning Statement

A positioning statement should include the name of the product or service (in the case of a new offering, why that name was chosen), the target market (including concrete information about the market), the benefits that will be emphasized in order to appeal to this target market, and the features that lend credibility to these benefits. All these points should be simply expressed, as in this hypothetical statement for Sprint Wireless:

> For growing, competitive businesses with a variety of communications needs [target market], Sprint Wireless [product name] is the voice, data, and video conferencing solution [features] that can help businesses expand in new directions [benefits].

Whether the positioning statement is for a brand, product, service, or some combination of these, the goal is the same: Provide a consistent message as you forge your place and image in the mind of the prospect. Exhibit 3-5 lists the procedure for developing a positioning statement.

Assess Creative Blueprints

You can and should play a key role in managing the creative focus of a brand, product, or service from a broader perspective, even though putting together a creative blueprint may also be the responsibility of a brand manager or a marketing communications manager. Examine all the blueprints to make sure they support the central images of products, product lines, brand identities, division identities, and even corporate identity. This evaluation is easier if everyone uses a template that ensures that all key issues are taken into account. One effective template has five parts:

EXHIBIT 3-5
How to Develop a Positioning Statement

1. Start with a solid understanding of your prospect and customers.
   - Who are they? Size of company, industry, type of business, their key success factors, and so on.
   - What do they think about your brand and about other brands in your category?
   - What problems or needs do they have that your brand can meet?
   - What are the goals and aspirations within this company?
   - What other companies are their role models?
   - What do they value for their customers: providing service? providing high value?
   - What factors influence the selection of a brand in your category?
   - Who influences the purchase decision in the companies you are targeting?
   - What events or other factors drive usage of your product, such as availability, timely delivery, high quality?
   - What prevents prospects from selecting your brand or purchasing a product in your category?
   - Does any well-known company that can serve as a role model or as an endorser use your product?
2. Make a competitive analysis.
   - How do your competitors position their brands?
   - What position or gap remains in the marketplace?
3. Make certain choices.
   - Who is your target market?
   - What is your single most important benefit or idea?
   - What features support the benefit or idea?
4. The statement is relevant; it addresses a need or value that is important to your target market.
5. The statement is easily communicated and understood.
6. The statement is original, ownable, and sustainable.
7. The statement provides clear and specific directions for all marketing communications elements.

1. Describe the target market.
2. List product or service benefits in customer terms.
3. Support these benefits. Note the features that provide these benefits and how the benefits can be convincingly communicated to potential customers.
4. Clearly describe the image that all creative activities will foster.
5. Provide an overview of the mix that will be used (advertising, public relations, promotion, direct sales, and so on), including projected spending for each.

By looking at the image each blueprint plans to project, you can quickly make sure that everything fits together smoothly. And by comparing overviews of the mix, which covers spending projections, you can think through how resources will ultimately be allocated among products, brands, and divisions.

Evaluate Marketing Communications

It is definitely important to remember that your main role is product strategy and business analysis, not copywriting or art direction. Nevertheless, it is your responsibility to make sure that the creative process produces messages that faithfully execute the strategy and adhere to the philosophy and values of the company.

The CLC approach goes a long way toward converting the creative process from a nearly mystical activity to a business process subject to analysis and rules. Here is a set of questions to guide your analysis of any marketing communications piece—particularly advertising—that is brought to you. It is your job to ask these. Answering them with copy, graphics, and innovative ideas is the role of the creative team.

1. Do I understand this communication? Confusion can arise if there are too many or too few ideas, words, visuals, or other components.
2. What is the strategy behind this communication? Does it fit in with other aspects of our marketing strategy?
3. Is there a Big Idea here? What is it? The acid test is whether an idea can be used for 30 years and still be fresh and interesting.
4. Is there a selling idea, a call to action, a clear reason the customer should buy this product or service?
5. Is the product the hero? If so, its name, features, and benefits will be clear.
6. Does this communication clearly identify the brand or, in the case of an unbranded product, the company name? Brand or company name support the integrity of the marketing communication.

Do not worry whether you like this particular communication. You are not the target for this piece.[2]

The Resultrek Web site (www.resultrek.com) provides examples of how expert marketers have answered these questions for current print and television advertisements. At the Web site, click on "Can this ad be saved?" for more information about using these questions and to compare your opinions with others.

Evaluate Media Plans

Media planning is yet another responsibility of brand or communications managers, often supported by advertising agencies and sometimes special media consultants. You must make sure that these important questions are answered by each plan.

1. Does the plan clearly identify how decisions are made in the target companies and whose attention is being sought? Investment in a piece of equipment, for example, may be the responsibility of the factory foreman in some situations, of the vice president for finance in others. Is the right person being targeted by the media plan? Is there support for the identification of this person as the decision maker?

2. Does the plan draw on a variety of media as appropriate? Plans tend to focus on one or two media because these have been used historically, are used by competition, appeal to the advertising agency, and so forth. A wide range of outlets can be effective in reaching key decision makers, and not all are traditional. R.W. Beck's use of market research to build awareness is a perfect example.

3. Does the creative approach fit with the media chosen? Does it all work together to support the image and the identity that you want this product to project?

4. Does the plan allow enough spending? Underfunding ensures that awareness will not be achieved and that the money invested will be wasted.

How Much Advertising Is Enough?

Your positioning statement provides part of the information you need to determine how much advertising to do. First, it identifies your targets, which means that research has been done on the size of that population. Second, it describes your intended

---

[2]These questions are based on Chapter 2 of Ogilvie (1985).

message, and if it is complicated, it will need to be repeated often. Aside from these two considerations, at least six other factors affect advertising decisions in Step Two of the CLC.

Factor One: Importance

How important is your message to prospects? If your product or service solves a problem that affects their annual pay bonus or the profitability of their company, they will work to learn more about you and your solution. If you offer a low-involvement product, you will need to tell your story several times before it sticks.

Factor Two: How Responsive Is the Product or Service to Advertising?

Certain products or services respond more readily to awareness-building campaigns than others. If yours is not very responsive, you may need to use other communication components as substitutes for advertising or to make it more effective. For example, WorldCom's approach was multidimensional.

Just before it acquired MCI, WorldCom launched a corporate advertising campaign with Michael Jordan as a spokesman, for consumer as well as business-to-business markets. The company waited for a sales increase, but it did not come. Before marketers could determine why, WorldCom announced acquisition of MCI, a significantly more visible company. Suddenly, the business-to-business sales force could open doors hitherto closed. Press coverage of the impending merger, combined with positive depictions of WorldCom as an aggressive, up-and-coming company, raised awareness among business customers in a way that advertising alone could not.

Factor Three: Dealing with Clutter

Some categories of products and services are cluttered with communications, whether a new technology or a mature product with tight competition. Getting noticed will require more spending, both in absolute terms and perhaps as a percentage of revenue. Especially in these cases, if you do not spend enough, everything you do spend is virtually wasted.

Factor Four: Is This a Special Needs Situation?

When there are specific awareness and communications barriers to overcome, crossing this hurdle can be expensive.

Examples are highly technical products that need a lot of support and explanation and a service in a highly competitive environment. Also, new offerings start with zero awareness and may need considerable investment to get off the ground.

Factor Five: How Good Are Your Advertisements?

How creative and effective are your communications? There is no handy formula for making great advertisements. In the early 1990s, Apple Computer's "1984" advertisement introduced the Macintosh. It ran only once, albeit during the Super Bowl. It generated a great deal of interest in the new product, and in 2001 it was still rated by viewers as one of the top-100 memorable television advertisements of the past 30 years.[3]

A great advertisement is known by its performance. It cuts through advertising clutter and sells. A good advertisement hammers away. A poor advertisement wastes budget.

Factor Six: How Much Synergy Can You Develop?

The experiences of BellSouth, R.W. Beck, and Accenture demonstrate how communication tools can increase the productivity of the direct sales force. Every time you add another kind of tool, the productivity of those you are already using goes up. Just as all communication must work toward building the total image or brand of a company, so must all aspects of communication be developed with this synergistic potential in mind. Print advertisements can be designed to support a promotion. The company Web site should be identified in all corporate communications—advertisements, packaging, banners at trade shows. By building on every opportunity for synergy, a company can increase awareness efficiently while enhancing brand and corporate identity.

Pfizer's approach to selling Zithromax, an antibiotic for children's ear infections, is an excellent example of communications synergy. A zebra was selected as the Zithromax "mascot," and Pfizer wrapped medical journals in zebra-striped paper, distributed stuffed zebras to pediatricians to use with their patients, donated a zebra to the San Francisco Zoo, sponsored a season of Sesame Street, and donated Zithromax in developing countries.

---

[3]"The 100 Greatest TV Ads," (accessed May 9, 2003), available at http://www.channel4.com/entertainment/tv/microsites/G/greatest/tv_ads/results.html.

In addition, Pfizer advertised to parents, encouraging them to ask for Zithromax ("Just five doses and you're done" tells parents they will have an easier time getting their children to complete the medication); to physicians; to children through the KidsEars.com Web site; and to families through a Children's Television Workshop magazine. The company's direct sales force (20,000 people worldwide) was supported by various efforts: toll-free numbers doctors could call for information on antibiotics, education programs for doctors, and presentations at international scientific conferences, which emphasized "The tissue is the issue" to differentiate the product. One promotional technique was to distribute rubber ink stamps to doctors to make it easier for them to write Zithromax prescriptions.

Pfizer is one of the largest drug manufacturers in the United States, and Zithromax is a strong product. Doctors write more than 60,000 prescriptions for Zithromax annually, compared with about 30,000 for the other leading prescription drug in its category.[4]

ADD ELECTRONIC TOOLS TO YOUR COMMUNICATIONS MIX

In business-to-business marketing, many companies use the Web to develop or improve customer access to their products or services, which is Step Three of the CLC. But in Step Two there are ways to build awareness using electronic tools, and some of these have the unique advantage of customizing the message for every prospect at a cost lower than advertising. When thinking through all aspects of using e-awareness, you should determine the fit between how target customers use all aspects of electronic communication and the offerings and investments your company can make. Here are some specific ideas for using electronic media as an awareness-building tool.

E-Tip I: Use What You Already Have

Visit your own Web site and think about both how it looks and what fresh ideas you can incorporate. Do you provide reasons for choosing your product over the competition? A good Web site makes it easy for visitors to gather more information on a topic

---

[4]"What's Black and White and Sells Medicine?" *New York Times*, (August 27, 2000), B1, B11.

that interests them and entices them to learn about your products or services and their benefits.

Because it can be relatively inexpensive to develop and maintain a professional-looking Web site, even small companies can compete with the behemoths. Unlike advertisements in *USA Today*, Web sites are well within the budget of everyone. As two computer-literate dogs in a *New Yorker* cartoon observed: "On the Web, nobody can tell you're a dog." No one can tell whether you are a small company or a new player in the business-to-business game.

E-Tip 2: Maximize Flexibility

A well-designed Web site can encourage prospects to choose how to obtain information. That is, they can customize the communication process—obtain detail if they want it or an overview if they do not. Make sure your Web site is flexible enough to meet the needs of many different types of visitors.

E-Tip 3: Create Dialogue with Targets

Two ways to create dialogue with customers are to communicate with them regularly through e-mail and to use your Web site as a tool for dialogue. Linda Rossetti, founder of the Internet consulting company eMaven, said at a Harvard Business School presentation: "Dialogue is an often forgotten and enormous enabler of results on a Web site. Stopping at the dialogue stage and enabling dialogue with some key customers or business partners can be more meaningful in terms of business results to the company earlier than commerce itself."[5]

To use e-mail productively, you need to gather addresses for prospects and create and implement a plan for communicating with them. That plan may include market research. Traditional business-to-business marketers listen by creating user panels—a dozen major customers who meet periodically to comment on marketing plans and provide feedback. The Internet enables you to establish numerous panels, each with a different slant or appli-

---

[5]"Getting It Wrong and Getting It Right in E-Commerce," *Harvard Business School Working Knowledge*, (posted May 2, 2000), (accessed May 9, 2003), available at http://hbsworkingknowledge.hbs.edu/item.jhtml?id=1475&t=strategy.

cation. You can receive customer feedback on new products, services, or marketing programs within hours.

E-Tip 4: Provide Support and Service

E-mail and Web sites afford another opportunity to offer support and service to potential or current customers. This is a way both to increase their awareness and to set the stage for an enhanced buyer relationship. Provide links to other Web sites that may be of interest to customers or a window with an annotated bibliography of recent important articles and books. This may convey to a customer that the company wants to provide benefits, a feeling that often carries over into perceiving benefits in products or services themselves.

E-Tip 5: Be an Educator

Online seminars and other Web-based training are strong tools for developing in-depth awareness of a product or service. They also enhance the customer's ability to derive value from your offerings.

E-Tip 6: Keep the Fresh Ideas Coming

Your Web site can and should provide something new every week or even every day to build awareness and interest in your product or service among current customers as well as prospects. Because the Web is so flexible and because ongoing relationships with customers and prospects are so important, constantly refreshing your Web site can be one of the strongest awareness-building tools you have, whether your company is large or small.

E-Tip 7: Use Viral Marketing to Spread the Positive

According to Ian Mount (2000), if you can "infect" a group of just 8% of Internet users with information about your company, this group will ultimately help you reach another 66%. Given the large and growing number of regular Web users, even a product with a narrow target audience can benefit from this kind of awareness-building, which is "passed along, from one user to another, just like a virus." The more carefully you identify the initial group with whom you establish contact, the more likely you are to infect your prospects. But be careful: "Once bad buzz gains online momentum, it's harder to stop than its offline brethren." (For other sources of information about viral marketing that could be helpful, see the "Notes" section at the end of this chapter.)

MEASURING AWARENESS OF BENEFITS

The CLC's mathematical model demands a number at the second learning gate: the percentage of your potential market that has learned not only that your product exists but also why they should buy it rather than competitors' solutions. It can be a challenge to pin down this number, but useful information is usually available in some form. Begin by tapping the measurements you have and create a learning plan to deepen your insights on an ongoing basis.

Exhibit 3-6 lists the kind of information you may already have, along with comments and caveats about using it to assess awareness from the CLC point of view. Even if your company does not have relevant research, perhaps because the marketing budget severely limits the amount that can be funded, several options are still available. Advertising agencies often track information for clients; you may be able to persuade yours to do the research at a reasonable fee, especially if the findings will influence how much money you invest with that agency. A subscription to a tracking service may help firm up your numbers at less cost than in-house research, though these services often provide information that is too broad. Consulting firm publications or online secondary sources can be useful if all else fails.

One solution looks easy but should always be taken with a grain of salt: Ask the sales force for information. True, sales personnel often have a good feel for what is happening, but they face two problems in gathering accurate data. First, it may be difficult for them to overcome their own biases, which reflect how hard their selling task seems to them. For example: "Awareness must be really low—I'd say about 10%—because it's so hard to get in the door of prospective customers." Second, they are dealing with a preselected sample, that is, people with whom they have some contact or an established relationship. Asking what they think about a new advertising campaign is not the same as asking a potential customer who has never even heard of your company. Keep in mind that factual, objective, and sometimes expensive research will never be a waste of time and money.

SUMMARY OF STEP TWO: BUILDING AWARENESS

First, although a direct sales force can do a lot for business-to-business companies, that alone is often neither the most effec-

EXHIBIT 3-6
Using Research Information to Measure Awareness

Measure	Question	Comments
Ad recall	Unaided: "How many ads can you recall seeing over the past 48 hours? Which ones stand out in your thought?" Aided: "Do you recall seeing the ad that...."	Advertising agency favorite. Caveat: You get what you measure. People may remember an ad but not who ran it.
Brand awareness	Unaided: "When you think of [product category], what companies come to mind?" Aided: [For those who did not name your company] "Did you know that [company name] also provides [product category]?"	Another agency favorite. Brand awareness gets the prospect only part way through the second learning gate.
Brand attributes	Focus group discussion: "When I say [product name], what attributes come to mind?"	This is closer to what we mean by awareness of benefits, but findings are not projectable.
Choice set	Unprompted: "The last time you purchased [product category], which suppliers did you consider? What were the strengths of each?" Prompted: "Did you consider [product name]? Why or why not?"	The follow-up question hits the bulls-eye, but the first crosses over into access and motivation. Anyone who considers your product is of interest, but the converse is not true: Failure to consider it may not be an awareness problem.
Digital dialogue	Threaded discussions or e-mail surveys offer a way to gain a thorough understanding of the market's level of knowledge.	Although e-mail surveys are becoming more common, you need to be careful about nonresponse bias. Your buyer may be low in the organization or out on the factory floor and may not regularly access e-mail. Or if your buyer is older than 55 years of age and high enough in the organization to have an assistant, he or she may be screened from the Web.

tive nor the most cost-efficient method for building optimal levels of awareness.

Second, other marketing communications tools—advertising, direct mail, telemarketing, public relations, and electronic media—can enhance personal selling enormously. The secret is to fit the medium to the target customer and to spend enough money on these support functions to have a meaningful effect on potential buyers.

Third, branding can be a powerful way to enhance awareness. It shortcuts the learning process about your product and its benefits, which is at the heart of the CLC.

Fourth, hands-on marketing managers are responsible for many awareness-building decisions, but strategic marketers play an important role in coordinating, balancing, and evaluating both the effectiveness of individual communications and the ideal blend of various communication tools.

Fifth, electronic modes vary in cost, flexibility, and fit with other components of the marketing mix. The company that overlooks electronic communication is missing attractive and often highly economical opportunities to enhance customer or prospect awareness.

Sixth, just as in Step One, measurement is vital if the CLC is going to be used effectively. Again, research is necessary to determine current levels of awareness, the likely effectiveness of awareness-building programs, and the success of these programs after they are implemented.

Notes

Brand Leadership by David A. Aaker and Erich Joachimsthaler (The Free Press, 2000) presents a clear and current assessment of the value of branding and ways to create strong brands.

Al Ries and Jack Trout's book, *Positioning: The Battle for Your Mind* (McGraw Hill, 2000), offers an excellent perspective on positioning in various marketing situations. Another useful resource is *The Brand Marketing Book* by Joe Marconi (American Marketing Association/McGraw Hill, 1999).

An excellent source of current resources on viral marketing is at the Economy.com Web site (http://www.economy.com/). Click on "Viral" for recent articles in such varied periodicals as *Fortune* and *Advertising Age*. A related book of interest is *Virus of the Mind: The New Science of the Meme* by Richard Brodie (Integral Press, 1995). Although this book does not address "viral marketing" per se, it discusses how ideas spread from one person to another, including ideas about businesses and business products.

Chapter 4

Who Can Access Your Product or Service?

What could be worse than an enthusiastic prospect, fully aware of your product's benefits and eager to buy, who does not have access to what you are selling? The focus of Step Three of the Customer Learning Curve is to make sure customers are not denied opportunities to buy your product or service. From the customer's point of view, the access issue is straightforward: Can I buy what I want, when I want, where I want? But from the marketer's perspective, access problems come in four different forms, any one of which can stymie an informed, interested prospect.

First, a company may have a traditional channel problem. Your prospect learns about what you are selling and its value proposition, decides to try it, and goes looking for your product but cannot find it. If the product is not a necessity, it may never be bought at all. But if the prospect's need is pressing, he or she will probably buy a competitor's product, which gives another company the benefit of your investment in building awareness. In this case, your prospect has been "switched in the channel."

Second, a company may have a capital deployment problem. This occurs primarily in service delivery situations and is even more basic than the problem of joining seller and buyer in one place. The infrastructure that must deliver the service is not in place. Consider digital subscriber line (DSL) access for high-speed Internet transmission. Without the expensive electronic equipment in the provider's central office, the service is not physically available. Usually the reason is capital investment shortfalls. In the case of DSL, for example, the dollar investment required for the infrastructure is so high that it strains the resources of even cash-rich telephone companies.

Third, and a bit more subtle, is the know-how problem. You are selling software, but your prospects are afraid their company will never learn how to use it correctly. Knowledge barriers can prevent access just as effectively as a lack of physical availability.

Fourth, a competitive relationship problem does not concern the buyer but is strictly an issue from the selling company's point of view. The buyer has access to your product or service, but the need is already being met by a competitor. In effect, your company does not have access to the buyer because of this prior relationship.

Any access problem is serious and must be addressed. The growth of the Internet has led many companies to focus on e-commerce as the first solution, but the Internet is not a cure-all. You need to identify which kind of access problem you have and then consider whether e-commerce or a more traditional approach will solve it.

In the following sections, we explore the challenges of each type of access problem and provide varied solutions to these challenges. Then we examine e-commerce in terms of access issues, a perspective every company needs to keep in mind.

TRADITIONAL CHANNEL PROBLEMS AND SOLUTIONS

As products, services, and industries go through stages in their life cycle, the optimal marketing strategy, especially the channel strategy, changes. In the introduction phase, an unfamiliar product or service needs help—extra services, complementary products, customer education. Companies often rely on a "missionary" sales force that can answer questions, customize products or services, provide feedback, and get customers over the hump of trying the new and different. Sometimes this is the only choice because others in the chain of distribution are not willing or able to support the new product or service.

In the growth stage, when demand is exploding, companies often expand access. Outsiders—sales representatives, agents, resellers, and wholesalers—give increasingly self-sufficient customers access where they want it.

In the maturity stage, competition intensifies, channels proliferate, and conflicts among channels ensue. As margins shrink, the direct sales force and the more expensive intermediaries are pared back. The lower cost and measurable results of direct marketing favor this option.

In the decline stage, creative marketers look for ways to reinvigorate their product or service: product or line extensions, new and improved versions, new applications, or repositioning. As at the beginning of the product life cycle, no one may be willing to sell the offering, so by default the direct sales force is the answer. Market niches become narrower and more specialized, and the sales force is asked to customize the offering on the spot to keep sales coming. Alternatively, declining products or services may become temporary cash cows because high-cost competitors pull out of the shrinking marketplace and loyal customers persist. In this case, if access is easy and comfortable, the decline may be "golden years" of profitability.

Here is how one company faced these life cycle challenges over a long period and how the changes influenced its ability to respond to challenges in Step Three—access to customers. In the 1950s, Miller Fluid Power created a new type of tie rod hydraulic cylinder that was easy to take apart, repair, and adjust; previously, cylinders needed to be discarded if faulty. Anticipating customer resistance to something so new, Miller handled its own distribution and customer education during the introductory phase. The company president, Frank Flick, took the show on the road in a large Cadillac with an Airstream trailer in tow, emblazoned with "College of Cylinder Knowledge." Flick visited potential users and provided both product information and demonstrations of how the cylinders could be used in their own businesses.

As the market grew, Miller replaced the direct sales force with distributors but continued its educational approach. When a new factory was built, for example, it included a training facility and living quarters for customers who came to learn how to use the redesigned cylinders.

Competition increased during the mature phase. Flick's first response was to cut back on direct education but return to a direct sales force that could still educate customers. Then a major competitor reduced its cylinder prices and began cutting into Miller's share of the market. The competitor did this by eliminating the education function and selling through industrial distributors, passing the distribution savings on to customers.

Unfortunately, Flick was reluctant to cut back his sales force and dispense with the educational component, though it was no longer needed by most customers. Miller's prices stayed high, and share continued to decline. Eventually, the business was acquired by a company that reduced the internal sales force, broadened the channels of distribution to include those used by the competition, and added telemarketing for accounts that required little service other than reorders. By realigning the business with its place in the product life cycle, the new owners improved performance in Step Three of the CLC and put the business back in the black.

A new stage in the product life cycle can clearly signal the need to think through current channel options and their suitability for the future. There are two approaches for handling the transition effectively: becoming customer driven and adding e-commerce to the arsenal.

Channel Solution 1: Be Customer Driven

In the late 1980s, two distribution experts, Louis Stern and Frederick Sturdivant (1987), proposed a model for updating access systems. Although the end result may look different from what would have emerged in 1987, the approach still makes a lot of sense.

1. Use market research to determine exactly what customers want in terms of access to your product or service. Research should be open-ended enough to allow customers to think about options that may not be currently used in your industry. Today, access options change quickly.
2. In an internal ideation session, brainstorm how an ideal system would look, one that takes into account both customer desires and the company's wishes. It may not be realistic to replace the entire sales force with people who have a doctorate in physics and an MBA, but realism is not the goal here. Open up thinking.
3. Take a hard look at the current situation. What are your strengths and weaknesses relative to where you would like to be? Are there obvious steps to take, such as replacing underperforming sales personnel, or steps your company has been postponing?
4. Assess what is feasible and possible to do in the current corporate environment, given time, money, and legal constraints. Within these limits, identify ways to incorporate the ideal.
5. Implement the new system as quickly as possible.

That is how Stern and Sturdivant approached the issue more than a decade ago, and the approach still works well, with one important caveat. Given the pressures of e-commerce, global competition, and shareholder demands for high performance in the competition for capital funding, companies must expand their thinking about what is feasible and possible. There can be no sacred cows in the competitive twenty-first century. Legacy assets—including those in channels of distribution—may simply be too expensive from the competitive point of view. The pressure to stand pat may be intense, but if change is required to keep pace with the market, you cannot afford to ignore your vision.

Channel Solution 2: Add E-Commerce to Your Access Arsenal

There is a place at each stage of the product life cycle for the addition of e-commerce components. Although it is especially important to consider these additions during transitions in the life cycle, even within each stage they can improve access and, consequently, sales and profits.

1. During introduction, your missionary sales force can be supported by rich information that is available electronically: through the company's Web site, online help desks, chat groups in which users exchange information, and e-mailed newsletters. This approach can establish a user community for early adopters, support educational activities of the sales force, and even provide invaluable feedback for debugging a product or service.

2. During growth, in-house electronic support for established customers may speed access at a lower cost, and savings can be passed on to customers. Online ordering, for example, may be attractive to some customers, especially those who place routine orders, are highly price sensitive, or want control.

3. During maturity, your company can support its margins without compromising customer service by using established (and paid for) e-commerce techniques, such as online ordering, or by pulling in new intermediaries who use e-commerce. Also, widen and deepen your focus by appealing to new narrow applications and niches through enhanced electronic support—rich information, help desk specialists, applications-specific chat groups, niche-focused e-mailed newsletters. Good support for these segments of customers can be an important differentiator in the highly competitive mature environment.

4. During decline, e-commerce can be added to or even replace traditional selling as it becomes uneconomical to employ a large sales force. E-commerce is a cost-efficient way to serve small and scattered user groups and even help them find new ways to use your product or service.

CAPITAL DEPLOYMENT PROBLEMS AND SOLUTIONS

As technology changes more and more rapidly, the magnitude of capital required to create access to a product or service can prove daunting even for a company with deep pockets. Capital deployment problems come in three forms, usually interrelated.

1. Financing: A large amount of capital is required to build a network such as DSL or start an airline.
2. Installation: It takes time to build or expand the physical infrastructure once the money is available.
3. System interdependence: A complete interactive system may be needed before any one component can be offered to customers. For example, even if a provider has DSL equipment in place, the modems in customers' homes must be fully operational before the lines can be used.

There are two tasks to undertake in dealing with these problems. The first is an internal marketing task: Justify capital expenditures to the organization by demonstrating that they will generate enough customer interest to yield an attractive rate of return. How can you make the case for this kind of investment?

For a start-up product or service, the situation is relatively straightforward and requires traditional financial analysis. In the case of expansion, the situation is different. Begin by implementing noncapital programs—marketing communications, public relations, sales force efforts, and Web initiatives customized to individual targets—to increase penetration in territories where access already exists. These areas are a kind of test market for the effect of marketing investments. If you can demonstrate that marketing support will achieve higher volume and profits in these areas, you can make the case for similar investment in new areas. Exhibit 4-1 presents a hypothetical case.

The second task is to build demand so that when the infrastructure is in place, customers are ready and willing to take advantage of the new access opportunities. Timing is critical: Presell to preempt a market, followed by rapid and intense awareness-building the moment the service goes live. Building awareness of a new business-to-business auction site, for example, should be timed so that interest peaks at the moment the site is accessible. As a precaution, make sure that marketers receive

EXHIBIT 4-1
How to Address Capital Deployment Problems in a Hypothetical Company

Currently, capital deployment in only 40% of the market leads to penetration of 1%.

100%

80% 40% 40% 60% 50% 60% 70% 60% = 1%

Raise capital deployment to 100%, and the new CLC looks like this (changes are in boldface). Penetration increases to 2.4%, but this is not large enough to justify the investment by this company.

100%

80% 40% **100%** 60% 50% 60% 70% 60% = 2.4%

Instead, the company works to improve noncapital marketing effectiveness. With marketing communications programs, media programs, and promotions that improve the numbers (in boldface) but do not change access, this is how the CLC looks.

100%

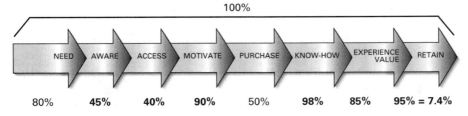

80% **45%** 40% **90%** 50% **98%** **85%** **95%** = 7.4%

When these improvements are supplemented by also increasing access to 100%, the new CLC indicates such a large increase in penetration (to 18.5%) that the investment can clearly be justified.

100%

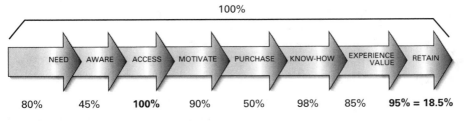

80% 45% **100%** 90% 50% 98% 85% **95%** = 18.5%

accurate information about timing, and build in plenty of leeway for deployment delays.

KNOW-HOW PROBLEMS AND SOLUTIONS

Business-to-business customers may be reluctant to try something new because they fear their company will never learn how to use it—that it will never pay off. Although the CLC addresses learning in Step Six, the issue in Step Three is not so much learning to use something new as it is the perception of possible difficulties.

One way around this frustrating situation is to think about customers' willingness to try new things and then develop targeted marketing programs that address different groups. Companies usually fall into the "adoption categories" that Everett Rogers (1983) describes in his marketing classic, *Diffusion of Innovation*.

- Innovators: The 2%–3% of buyers who are almost obsessed with anything new.
- Early adopters: Opinion leaders to whom most of us look to make true tests of new ideas and products.
- Early majority: People who deliberate, look at early adopters, and then decide whether to embrace the change.
- Late majority: Skeptics who are often driven to adopt simply to be able to participate with the world around them.
- Laggards: This is the "if it ain't broke, don't fix it" crowd.

Geoffrey Moore (1995; see also Moore and McKenna 1999) refers to the rapid diffusion of Silicon Valley products through the early majority stage as a "tornado of demand." Whether adoption is rapid or slow, a change agent can play a key role in the diffusion process. This is the person or company that does whatever is necessary to enable potential customers to use the innovation, regardless of their adoption profile. In many companies that are interested in introducing new technology, the role of change agent is played by the strategic marketer. Here are some approaches to use in bridging the know-how access gap.

Know-how Solution 1: Target Innovators and Early Adopters First

Innovators love to participate in beta tests, or even alpha tests, and delight in providing feedback on a new product or service. This feedback provides insights into all aspects of the CLC for a new offering and can give you a good idea about how the product or service may be used and who needs it. The information helps define benefits, an attractive price, a sales force approach, and even how to teach customers to use and obtain benefit from the offering.

For early adopters, Moore suggests that the marketer wrap the innovation in complementary products and services and position this package as the solution to an industry-specific problem. Unlike the innovators, who tend to make excuses for any shortcomings, early adopters will not tolerate finicky technology. They want a business problem solved, and they expect a turn-key product. By targeting these groups first, you can not only generate ideas for serving other categories of adopters but also begin building word of mouth that will pull in more conservative targets.

Know-how Solution 2: Educate or Do It for Them

As the target group widens, you must find ways to build know-how. Rogers (1983) points out that the more complex the innovation, the more knowledge is needed before it will be adopted. If marketers ignore this step, unhappy customers are likely to abandon the product. You can avoid this kind of rejection both by educating potential users and by creating virtually fail-safe methods for them to access and use a new product or service, which sets the stage for continued outreach into the more conservative purchase groups.

One Internet company offered its clients customer-satisfaction surveys ("digital dialogues"), with a revolutionary value proposition for market research. For less than 5% of the cost of traditional telephone or paper surveys, clients could obtain immediate feedback on customer satisfaction, complete with mail alerts to responsible managers when ratings were low and complete reports to management within 24 hours. Clients not only received fast feedback but also could afford to survey customers much more frequently, even after every transaction.

One of the first clients for this service was a leading human resources outsourcing company. From the technological point of view, the client could have used the new approach within three months of signing up, but the company was not filled with innovators or even early adopters. Management focused on the problems that might arise. Which of the four or five departments should receive the e-mail alerts? How could the organization meet higher customer expectations that an alert would be resolved quickly? Most significantly, would executive bonuses—based in part on the old paper surveys—be unpredictably affected by the change in method?

It took more than a year for the Internet company to educate the client about the benefits of the new approach. Marketing strategists used a combination of business process expertise, customer satisfaction technology, and thorough knowledge of the client's products and services to overcome the steep know-how barriers. Issues needed to be addressed one at a time, with patience and respect for corporate structure. The solution involved both "doing it for them" and educating the company about how to use the new service effectively.

From this experience, the Internet company found that overcoming such barriers was an important differentiating core competency as it competed against others in this field. The lesson? Solving the know-how problem not only is important to obtain product adoption but also can result in a significant advantage that is not easy for competitors to duplicate. A company that can overcome these barriers can move past limits to maximize its performance in Step Three of the CLC.

Know-how Solution 3: Use Electronic Communication to Educate and Support

Compaq University provides more than 30,000 online training courses each month for its employees. Most of the courses are video-illustrated guides for service technicians and technology primers on feature benefits for salespeople, complete with PowerPoint sales presentation shells. In another company, product managers include Web-based product briefings in their product and program launch packages. The information is available around the clock, and salespeople often access the briefings at 10 P.M. the night before they visit a customer. They take their laptop on sales calls and share sections of the internal material with customers.

Today, a heavy dose of electronic-based training is common for both employees and customers, ranging from detailed user instructions to education on concepts and business practices that complement the product or service packages. This training is one of the most effective and efficient tools for business-to-business marketers, but it is not automatically successful. As in every other field of marketing, there are keys to success in Web-based training.

- Electronic-based training must be easy, inviting, and even fun. Participants have the power to click off a boring presentation the moment it stops holding their interest. Instructional screens must have frequent interactions—a drag-and-drop exercise, a puzzle, a formula expressed as an analog slide bar—and there cannot be enough appropriate animation.
- The technology must be foolproof. If your target is not likely to have a great deal of bandwidth, put enabling technology on a CD-ROM and have just the interactivity portion on the Web.

People want to interact with other people. Pat LeFor, of the online learning group at Empire State University, says that participants in Internet courses report that they value what they learn from other participants, through threaded discussions and comparing posted homework assignments, even more than interaction with their instructors by e-mail.[1]

COMPETITIVE RELATIONSHIP PROBLEMS AND SOLUTIONS

When the competition has such a strong relationship with a potential customer that your access is effectively blocked, the first question to ask is: "How important is this customer or group of customers to me?" The second is: "How much time and energy are worth investing to win this customer over?" If the investment is greater than the payoff, the wisest strategy is to avoid direct confrontation and find opportunities elsewhere. Here are some effective strategies for dealing with competitive relationships.

Competitive Solution 1: Sidestep the Relationship by Finding Receptive Niches

Many successful, regional public accounting firms started as small, individual practices. As start-ups, they found it difficult to crack the carefully protected relationships that other accounting firms had with the most prominent corporations in their regions. A strategy that has proved successful time and again is to con-

---

[1]Personal communication to first author, May 2000.

centrate on small and mid-size companies—the less well-defended relationships—and serve them effectively, often with industry specialists. Some of these clients turn out to be baby whales, and when the whales grow up, the start-up firm has its own set of relationships among the largest and most prominent corporations, along with industry expertise, a reputation for professionalism and client service, and the stature to pursue new business in any corporation in its region.

The main lesson from this example is that going around the relationship is one way to compete successfully against firms that rely on strong relationships. By constantly succeeding among receptive clients, start-ups can overcome barriers to reaching potential customers.

Competitive Solution 2: Buy the Relationship

Early in the formation of a start-up venture, the company's chief operating officer (COO) identified a key client he wanted. Winning this client would provide not only needed revenue but also instant credibility in a highly competitive field. The prospect was already working with a provider that had recently added new capabilities to its product offerings, but this did not stop the COO. He found a salesperson who had a strong personal relationship with the president of the target company and hired him. Within a few months, he landed the client. For the price of a hire, the COO "bought" the relationship that was so important to his company's success.

In buying relationships, keep two things in mind. First, make sure the investment will deliver what you want. The start-up venture COO did some tactful investigation to make sure the salesperson had the kind of relationship with the target that he claimed to have. Second, make sure you do not pay more for the relationship than it is worth. Our start-up COO also looked at the track record of the salesperson to determine whether he would be an asset to the company in the long run.

Competitive Solution 3: Borrow the Relationship

A small California training and communications company had years of expertise in developing high-quality, effective training programs for large companies. Recently, it perfected the ability to create interesting and successful interactive online training programs. How could it expand its customer base to take advantage of this skill set while commanding top dollar for its offerings?

Rather than approach potential customers directly, the company formed a strategic alliance with a strong regional advertising agency. The trainers and the advertisers shared a communications philosophy, an organizational climate, and a set of values that made them natural allies. When the advertising agency found that clients needed training expertise, it introduced the partner, who did the same. Over several years, both companies flourished because they were able to borrow and build on the other's relationships with customers.

There are three considerations in forming these kinds of alliances. First, the potential partner must share a target customer base. Second, there must be enough commonalities between the two to ensure that clients who are comfortable with one company will be likely customers for the other. Third, any financial arrangements for referral fees, profit sharing, and so on must be clarified in advance, preferably by legal contract. If not, the alliance may work to the detriment of both parties.

Competitive Solution 4: Flank the Relationships

Rapid technological and market changes provide opportunities as well as challenges to strategic marketers. Look at the offerings of competitors to key customers you would like to win for yourself and identify some set of features or benefits that the competition does not provide. Through a technological improvement or a product twist, you may be able to offer an advantage. Perhaps you can ship product faster than competitors, or at lower cost, or in quantities or forms that are more attractive to the customer. Sometimes established suppliers are invested in older technology that puts them at a disadvantage. A flank attack works only if you can identify something new that customers need.

Competitive Solution 5: Exit the Segment

If you cannot win, leave the field. Redefine your target audience and reposition your product. Walk away from a losing battle and save resources for other contests you can win.

E-COMMERCE: LOW-COST ACCESS TO CUSTOMERS

Electronic commerce has radically changed access to business markets in many industries. It requires serious consideration as you look at your company's performance in Step Three of the CLC. Several trends are noteworthy.

Trend 1: Pruning for Value-Added Focus

The simplest use of e-commerce to gain access involves routine purchases. These require relatively little "selling," or minimal explanation of the product and its benefits, particularly if the buyer and seller have a standing relationship. A heavy equipment manufacturer that uses thousands of the same screws and bolts every month can easily see the advantage of ordering them electronically. If the manufacturer has flat production plans and the computer capability to create a standing order, so much the better. Intermediaries, such as a direct sales force or distributors, are not needed.

The key factor is whether the intermediary adds value. A sales visit may strengthen personal bonds, and these need to be assessed from an economic point of view. Unless there is a real benefit to the buyer, the intermediary may not be cost effective.

Trend 2: Auctions

E-commerce has made significant access inroads for highly specialized products (and sometimes services) with relatively few buyers and sellers. DoveBid, for example, may auction off the assets of a bankrupt pharmaceutical firm whose equipment is of interest to a small number of companies. By bringing together worldwide buyers through the Internet, DoveBid can create a market that would not be profitable to serve otherwise.

There is also an opportunity for price- and volume-oriented Internet auctioneers. For example, FairMarket and FreeMarkets bring together large numbers of buyers and sellers and primarily conduct "downward" auctions; they offer used assets, excess inventories, and all kinds of direct and indirect materials to the highest bidder. At times, they also conduct "upward" auctions: Buyers specify what they want, at what price, and wait for a seller to come forward.[2] For companies that want to unload branded merchandise as cost-efficiently as possible, these Internet marketplaces eliminate the need for salespeople or other intermediaries.

---

[2]*HBS Working Knowledge* (2000), "Market Makers Bid for Success," (accessed May 9, 2003), [available at http://hbsworkingknowledge.hbs.edu/item.jhtml?id=1540&t=technology].

In these three electronic access cases—routine ordering, specialized markets, and mass markets—sellers are not unwilling "victims" of e-commerce. Rather, e-commerce gives them wider access to buyers, reduces sales calls, and radically reduces the cost of customer access. In these situations, access is enhanced from the perspective of both buyers and sellers.

Trend 3: Buying Alliances

Recently, three large real estate services (CB Richard Ellis Services, Jones Lang LaSalle Inc., and Trammell Crow Co.) that manage 1.2 billion square feet of office space joined in an online buying alliance. This not only will increase their purchasing power but also will streamline ordering, reduce purchasing expenses, and facilitate inventory management (Rich 2000).

What Next?

Channels and consultative sales forces that add considerable value—through information, services, scale economies, and even social value—will continue to serve large business-to-business customers in complex transactions, but relationships with these customers will be enhanced electronically. For small and perhaps even middle-sized customers, e-commerce may provide better service and stronger relationships than overloaded call centers (Evans and Wurster 2000).

The potential for e-commerce highlights certain themes that all business-to-business marketers should consider for improving performance in Step Three of the CLC. First, intermediaries are increasingly vulnerable to elimination. The key is whether they add value. Second, no company can assume that its current distribution system is adequate, regardless of how much is invested in it or its success in the past. Indeed, maintaining this "legacy asset" may place a company in competitive danger. Every company should challenge itself to exploit e-commerce as a business asset. Third, providing customers with lots of information they have not been able to obtain easily in other ways may no longer be enough to keep them loyal. Internet search engines grow more sophisticated by the month, and new approaches make it much easier for surfers to find what they want and need to know.

Be alert to changes in business-to-business access that the Internet provides. This can help you anticipate what may happen next in your business and industry so you can avoid disasters.

Such vigilance also enables you to create ways to use e-commerce to enhance your position in the marketplace.

MEASURING ACCESS

In Step Three of the CLC, you must determine the percentage of the potential market with access to your product or service. Different measurements apply to different access situations.

In Traditional Channel Situations

In the case of traditional channel problems, you need to know where your target customers want and expect to access your product or service. Secondary sources, such as industry studies, may be sufficient, but sometimes primary research is needed to obtain a clear picture of your targets' preferred channels and the percentage of your product flowing through each.

Look at the channel arrangements you have in place, and use secondary research to estimate product accessibility among your target audience. Perhaps your company sells cabinetry to two market segments: home builders and home-improvement contractors. Secondary sources indicate that 80% of cabinetry sales to home builders are handled by sales force calls on company headquarters, and 20% are through the Internet. For home-improvement contractors, 90% of sales are through retailers such as Home Depot, and 10% are through the Internet.

It is a simple exercise to determine how your channel relationships match buyer expectations. Do you have a direct sales force for building companies? Does the geographic coverage of the sales force match the distribution of building companies? Is it effective in reaching these customers? Does your company sell through the Internet? If so, is it effective, well run, and widely publicized among building companies? The questions are different for the contractor group. Does your company have shelf space in retail outlets? Some or all? Can individual contractors find and access your Web site to make purchases there?

Primary research is needed when target definitions do not match the standard secondary research categories or when distribution patterns make it unclear where and how customers expect to access products or services. Focus groups, one-on-one interviews, surveys, and observations of purchasing patterns can provide important information on customer behavior, which then can be matched with the company's current systems to identify gaps.

In Capital Deployment Situations

When capital deployment is the issue, you can obtain internal information about physical deployment, by talking to the engineering or operations teams. After you determine where your services are deployed, you must measure access from the customer's point of view.

Let us say your service is deployed in 100 of 1000 central office buildings. It is tempting to assume that 10% of customers have service access. Rather than accept this easy answer, dig deeper.

- What percentage of target customers are served by the 100 office buildings? Perhaps these sites account for 50%—or only 2%—of your targets.
- What percentage of your sales are represented by the target customers who have access? Perhaps only 2% of your target customers have access, but they may account for 80% of your sales potential.

The key is to measure service penetration on the basis of whatever standards of success your company uses: number of customers served, percentage of customers served, dollar volume of sales to these customers, or profitability of sales to these customers.

In Know-how Situations

When know-how is the issue, first estimates can come from sales force feedback or straw polls in focus groups. If half the participants in a focus group say they would not buy your product because they do not think they could use it, you have a problem. For all its limitations, qualitative research alerts you to this fact, and you need to determine how large the problem is.

Quantitative surveys can probe the issue by asking customers and prospects to assess their own level of knowledge, but this approach has drawbacks. People who are afraid of a new technology are less likely to agree to be surveyed on the topic, or they may agree but are reluctant to admit their fears.

On-site observation can provide insight into what proportion of customers know how to use your product, but the issue is whether prospects think they know how to use it. Market trials of programs designed to overcome the know-how hurdle are another way to pin down the percentage of target companies in this category.

A combination of measures will be required: qualitative (to alert you to a problem), quantitative (to obtain a rough estimate of its magnitude), observation (to understand the realities), and market trials (to test solutions).

In Competitive Situations

Measurements of the potential market whose access to your product or service is obstructed by a relationship with your competitors will vary according to the strategies you use to handle the situation.

- If you buy access by hiring salespeople, measurement is straightforward: number of sales, dollar value of sales.
- If you borrow access through strategic alliances, you must assess the value created by the alliance. Is the value to each partner about the same? Is the extra value created by being in the alliance sufficiently greater than the value you could create on your own to justify the costs of maintaining the alliance?
- A flanking attack on the obstructing relationship calls for measuring "share of wallet."
- Marketing to niches requires measurement of niche size and share of the niche's volume.
- Exiting should be assessed by computing not only the volume of lost sales but also the hidden costs, such as losing profit contribution to overhead.

You must measure Web site access effectiveness by both quantitative and qualitative means. In the quantitative category are number of transactions, dollar volume of transactions, cost per transaction, and customer feedback on satisfaction with the site. Qualitative measures should gauge how well the site establishes and nurtures your relationship with customers.

ACCESS FROM THE CLC PERSPECTIVE

Every step of the CLC is connected to every other because customer learning is not a neat, linear process. When you focus on helping customers through any one of the steps, you gain insight into their thinking, which enables you to help them through all the steps and give them what they want and need. Here are some ways to integrate access issues into other steps of the CLC.

Consider Access an Important Aspect of Segmentation

In Step One—determining need—we noted that different customers may want the same thing but in different manifestations. For example, Dell serves companies that order thousands of computers a year and individuals who order two computers a decade. How customers want to access a product is an important aspect of market segmentation.

Build Access Awareness into General Awareness

Do you have a customer segment that wants to access your product or service through online ordering? If so, promote your Web site in basic awareness-building. Perhaps your primary targets want direct sales calls so that they can discuss the customized features they need. If you have a booth at a trade show to build product awareness, make sure it is staffed with your best salespeople—the kind of experts prospects want to see walk through their door.

Anticipate Future CLC Steps in Designing Access

Your product or service may require hands-on setup and instruction if the customer is going to learn to use it successfully and experience value. Online ordering may seem good in terms of access costs and may even meet the needs that customers think they have. But if your research reveals that support will be needed down the line, create an access system that not only delivers your product or service but also moves it through later stages of the CLC.

Maximize Sales Force Effectiveness Throughout the CLC

A powerful asset in providing customers with access to your product or service is the direct sales force. It also may have a role to play in building awareness, motivating customers to buy, teaching customers to use the product, or helping them experience satisfaction. The sales force often is invaluable in closing a sale, as well as in the repurchase or continued usage stage.

At each step of the CLC, think about how to use the sales force most effectively. Should a master at closing multimillion-dollar sales be the same person who delivers a product that requires several hours to set up and demonstrate? Could that role be played by someone else? Perhaps the stellar salesperson should arrive with the product and a tech support specialist, introduce the customer, and exit gracefully.

A good sales force is not a homogeneous group. Individuals have different strengths and weaknesses, areas of expertise, and tasks they enjoy. Consider how well the overall sales force job description and the skills of individuals or groups of salespeople match the unique needs of your target markets. A good match can optimize your investment in direct selling, support the entire CLC effectively, and ultimately increase sales and profits substantially. (We address sales force issues in Chapter 6.)

SUMMARY OF STEP THREE: ACCESS

First, if your company has a traditional access problem—channels, capital deployment, know-how, or competitive relationship barriers—count yourself lucky. Its solution can yield in a matter of months or quarters the same results that might take years of product development, awareness-building, and/or sales force effort.

Second, electronic commerce is changing things, and the company that ignores this does so at its own peril. Yet, e-commerce is not changing everything, and e-marketing does not solve every problem. Because it can be expensive and time consuming to create electronic access, companies should think it through and plan strategically. A knee-jerk reaction can be costly and ineffective.

Third, customer expectations for access are rising, due not only to e-commerce but also to other changes in the marketing environment. There are many new opportunities for companies to form partnerships with their customers, both to improve access and to gain a competitive advantage that can serve them well in the future.

Fourth, access solutions must be integrated with one another and with other steps in the CLC to enhance the customer's total learning experience and create a customer base with strong loyalty.

Chapter 5

Are Your Customers Motivated?

Motivation is Step Four in the Customer Learning Curve process. A prospect must need what you are selling, be aware of it, and have access to it, but without motivation there will be no purchase. In business-to-business marketing, examples of motivated prospects are a company that qualifies yours to be one of the final three or four bidders asked to make a proposal, a buyer who agrees to visit another customer's site to see your heavy equipment in action, or someone who signs on for a free demonstration or sample of your computer software. Motivation is all about overcoming inertia, breaking old habits, and getting a prospect to devote an unusual level of attention and energy to your product or service.

If your offering is central to your customer's business, it can be the focus of the motivational program—free samples, visits to your factory, free training to extract more value from your offering, and so forth. More often the product or service plays a secondary or even marginal role, and something extra is needed to overcome the prospect's inertia.

A marketer who wants to motivate business-to-business customers should answer several questions.

- Who in the target company should be motivated? Who is the true decision maker?
- What will interest and excite that person? The product or service itself? Something else that can be associated with the offering to provide motivation?
- What holds the prospect back? Habit? Inertia? An overloaded schedule?
- How can the answers to these questions be combined to arrive at a motivational program that works?

WHO SHOULD BE MOTIVATED?

Pinpointing the person to motivate may not be easy. Even for a single product in a single target segment, there can be a wide variety of decision makers. For example, UPS Next Day Air delivery service must appeal to a wide range of people in different corporations. In large companies, several administrative assistants may choose which service to use according to personal preference, or a purchasing agent may sign an annual contract with a single supplier. In other companies, the mail room staff chooses the service. In small businesses, the decision maker may be the office assistant or the owner.

It is especially important to identify the target in Step Four because various decision makers may be motivated differently. How can marketers do this? In the case of large accounts or contracts, the sales force probably can provide valuable information. The only caveat is that sometimes salespeople, especially those with less experience, misidentify key players and overestimate the decision-making power of the people they know. A senior executive at ADP remarked to one of the authors: "Our new salespeople often sell low and service low and can miss an entire level in the payroll outsourcing decision-making process."

When there is little sales force interaction or when many small decisions are made daily (as in the UPS situation), market research is the only practical way to determine who makes the buying decision. A mail, telephone, or online survey of purchasing departments at companies with more than 1000 employees could ask: "Who makes the decisions in your company regarding overnight shipping of small packages?" "Are decisions left to individuals or made on a corporate level?" A compilation of results may reveal that most companies in the aerospace industry use contracts, or most advertising agencies leave overnight shipping decisions to the administrative staff. This information is helpful in designing marketing campaigns or in directing salespeople. The findings also can be entered into a database for personalized direct mail or e-mail.

WHAT EXCITES THE DECISION MAKER?

The chief factor to consider in determining how to appeal to each type of decision maker is, How important is your product in the decision maker's business? If it is critical, the motivational program can center around what you are selling. Psychologists call such programs—free samples, visits to your factory, free value-added training, and so forth—*intrinsic* motivators.

Many business-to-business purchases have intrinsic interest simply because so much money is at stake, and a wise decision reflects on the performance of the decision maker. If a person's job performance depends on selecting an economical computer system that performs faultlessly, the product's features and benefits are intrinsically interesting. In other cases, products are just plain captivating. A programmer who devotes a career to developing new software that runs faster and better is intrinsically interested in a new Intel chip that makes better program design possible. A new type of electrical generator is of intrinsic interest to engineers at power companies. And the Web seems to fascinate everyone.

In contrast, many purchases in the business-to-business world are not intrinsically interesting to most decision makers: yet another order of screws and bolts, a shipment of copier paper, or the delivery service for a low-priority package. Whether these purchases are valued at a few dollars or millions, there is nothing of intrinsic interest about the product or service. The challenge is to find a logical extrinsic motivator—a little extra value—to enhance sales. Both types of motivation are discussed next.

Intrinsic Motivation

Intrinsic motivation is direct, economical, and effective because the product makes its own sales pitch. Psychologist Alfie Kohn makes a compelling argument that intrinsic motivation is always far more powerful than extrinsic motivation. He contends that learning for the sake of learning is more effective than learning for grades and that making work more worthwhile is more effective than cash bonuses.

Dr. Kohn's lesson for marketers is this: If you have the possibility to use intrinsic motivation, if your product is important enough, don't pass it up and settle for its less effective cousin, extrinsic motivation. (For further information on motivation, see the "Notes" section at the end of this chapter.) Perhaps the best example of intrinsic motivation in marketing is to let the product sell itself through sampling, either direct or indirect.

Direct Sampling

Sampling is easy in low-value consumer marketing and can be practical in business-to-business situations as well. Some types of direct sampling are free trials, money-back guarantees, and piggybacking.

Free trials are a good choice when the product is easy to use, installation is minimal, and the risk of breakage is relatively small. Examples are copiers, fax machines, and telephones. Even complex products can be tried out if a technician is sent along to make sure the sample is installed and used properly and works right. Some companies offer such a trial for a month or more, with real success. Not only are any bugs worked out for the prospect, but the prospect has also invested time in the learning curve, which increases the willingness to buy.

Money-back guarantees for smaller purchases are, in effect, a form of sampling. Try it, and if you are not satisfied, we will refund the purchase price.

Piggyback sampling involves adding a product or service to one that already interests the target audience. When prepaid telephone cards were introduced, companies wanted to generate trial by upscale business travelers. They offered free cards to decision makers in target companies that contracted for premier long-distance service. Many began purchasing cards for their employees, and sales grew.

Three examples show how sampling can be expanded to give business-to-business customers first-hand experience with products or services. In each case, the result was improved performance for these companies in Step Four of the CLC.

1. Carolina Power and Light built a Customer Service Center that incorporated its own value-added products—special lighting, uninterrupted power, surge protection, and so forth. In this center was a large bay where service vehicles could be retrofitted, repaired, and loaded with service parts. The five sections of the bay were illuminated with different kinds of lights that CP&L offered to commercial customers for warehouses, factories, or other large buildings. Salespeople showed prospects how each kind of light looked and worked, pointed out the respective advantages, and followed up with a written comparison of benefits, installation and maintenance costs, repair history, energy use, and so forth. Although not a free trial, this kind of sampling gave the sales staff an opportunity to answer questions, overcome objections, and obtain a clear idea of buyer interest.

2. FMC's Food Tech group built a technology center that can simulate prospects' food processing lines. FMC can demonstrate how its equipment will improve productivity for the customer.

3. Emergency One, the leading manufacturer of fire trucks, invites fire chiefs to the factory in Ocala, Fla. The "sampling visit" impresses prospects with what Emergency One is doing for their peers and showcases the latest innovations.

A closely related approach is to take prospects to facilities not in their line of business where your product or service is used. These visits give them insight into what may be necessary in terms of layout, logistics, and personnel to make the product or service effective in their own setting. They also have an opportunity to gain information from another user, a noncompetitor who can be trusted to give an objective evaluation of the offering.

Indirect Sampling

Indirect sampling uses education to show potential customers what your company can do for them. For example, a small insurance firm in Monterey, Calif., has specialized knowledge regarding liability insurance for architects and building engineers. It established a general education program, a "Risk Management School," for potential clients. This enables the company to show its expertise, offer something of value to potential customers, and motivate purchase by offering liability insurance at a lower rate to those who implement the innovative, risk-reduction programs described in the school. The company not only attracts new customers but also benefits from fewer claims among "graduates." A workshop gives prospects a "sample" of what it might be like to convert their entire insurance relationship to this company.

Extrinsic Motivation

When a product or service does not intrinsically motivate buyers, the first extrinsic motivator that comes to mind is a price reduction. Yet price cuts or discounts have hidden costs that make them undesirable in many situations. A case in point is a large telecommunications company that wanted to increase international long-distance volume among its many business-to-business customers. Potential buyers identified the cost of international calls as a major barrier, so the product manager created a program for new subscribers that matched during the first quarter the best price offer of any other company. The company would still make a small margin on these calls, and customers were expected to remain loyal even when their bill returned to normal because the company offered excellent service, clear connections, and highly accurate billing.

What is wrong with this scenario? It worked in the short term—price promotions usually do. But it created a long-term headache: New customers came to expect low international rates and switched carriers when the price went up. They were not only more price sensitive but also more vulnerable to competitors' offers of low rates.

Direct price incentives may have a place in your arsenal, but they have several disadvantages. Price incentives are

- Always the most expensive promotion you can run;
- Significantly less effective at producing ongoing sales than sampling;
- Easily matched and therefore negated;
- Erosive of brand image: "Something's wrong with the product if it has to be discounted";
- Educational in a negative way, because customers are taught not to pay full price;
- Symptomatic of the product manager's fear that the price is too high;
- Easy substitute for the hard work of finding the real barrier to purchase; and
- Irrelevant if the barrier to purchase is not price.

Price incentives can be effective and useful, but only if price is the barrier to purchase and if all the incentive's costs are taken into account. For a specific example of the cost of a discount, see Exhibit 5-1.

A better approach to extrinsic motivation is to borrow on the products, problems, activities, and ideas that your prospects care about. A promotion that associates your product with an area of critical importance to prospects can be almost as effective as intrinsic motivation.

A good interest-borrowing promotion cuts through the clutter by tapping the issues that matter to the customer. A great interest-borrowing promotion builds a relationship with prospects by communicating that you understand them and are committed to helping them meet their most important needs. The story of one product that significantly improved its performance in Step Four of the CLC through extrinsic motivation, albeit in a business-to-consumer setting, is a true inspiration.

EXHIBIT 5-1
Discounts Are Expensive

If your net profit margin is 20%, a price discount of 10% cuts your profit in half.

	Base Case		Effect of 10% Discount	
Revenue	$10,000,000	100%	$9,000,000	100%
Cost of goods sold	$ 5,000,000	50%	$5,000,000	56%
Gross margin	$ 5,000,000	50%	$4,000,000	44%
Expenses	$ 3,000,000	30%	$3,000,000	33%
Net profit	**$ 2,000,000**	20%	**$1,000,000**	11%

The soft drink market is brutally competitive, and the major brands, with the largest marketing budgets, rule the world. This is particularly true in the prime target group of preteens and teenagers, whose consumption is extremely high and whose brand loyalty today translates into heavy sales for years to come. Enter Sundrop, a regional product owned by Procter & Gamble. There were no plans for rollout and a minuscule advertising budget with which to build share and volume. The product manager began by focusing on rural North Carolina, where Sundrop had good distribution.

Sundrop's major product characteristics are sweet flavor and caffeine fortification. It appeals especially to youths 10 to 14 years of age, and the marketing team determined what was really important in the lives of these kids: baseball. They then developed a simple program. Sundrop proofs-of-purchase could be exchanged for Louisville Slugger baseball equipment—bats, mitts, and balls. These were donated by the manufacturer, which saw the value of such low-cost advertising and goodwill. All the Little Leaguer parents in the Sundrop territory received letters announcing the program and encouraging their family to participate.

The program succeeded beyond the company's wildest expectations. Whole communities participated in order to equip their local team. Louisville Slugger needed to ask for financial assistance from Sundrop to fulfill orders. Sundrop was delighted to comply—it had sold thousands of gallons of soda as a result of the promotion. At that point, additional promotional expense could be justified.

When faced with a particularly difficult business-to-business motivation problem, it pays to think about what interests your prospects. Here are some practical approaches for integrating extrinsic motivation into business-to-business marketing.

Borrow on Self-Interest

Stu Kahn, the head of a major accounting firm's litigation accounting practice, created an excellent program to increase the number of litigator clients. The company had developed a multi-million-dollar practice in New York City the old fashioned way— by nurturing relationships with litigators, doing excellent work, and earning referrals. But partners in other cities found it impossible to get appointments with their local star litigators. To solve this problem, Kahn's first step was to learn about the targets by interviewing litigators.

The first finding was that litigators are too busy to be surveyed. Most interviews had to be conducted before 7 A.M., after 6 P.M., or on Sundays. The incentive that finally worked was a contribution to the charity of the litigator's choice. The second finding was that litigators almost never think about litigation accounting. To them it is a detail. They are the stars; litigation accounting is the supporting cast.

The survey revealed that for most respondents the most important issue is "growing my practice"—in other words, marketing. Kahn then surveyed the clients that litigators hope to reach: corporate counsels. Based on the results, a graphic-rich presentation was prepared, and Kahn coached ten partners around the country on how to deliver it.

The promise to show litigators how to build their practice with corporate counsels assured entry into the partners' meeting of every law firm targeted. The presentation, which detailed the results of the corporate counsel survey, included only a single slide about the accounting firm; it reported that among corporate counsels, the firm's litigation accounting services had the highest quality ratings. This foot in the door enabled Kahn's team to gain appointments with prospects. They then used traditional techniques to build relationships and develop the practice.

Kahn's program illustrates how business-to-business marketers can learn what their prospects care about and borrow on those concerns. Note another key success factor: Kahn did not ask the promotion to do everything. On the contrary, it helped the local partner overcome just one obstacle: getting an audience with the star.

Get Specific

Great motivation programs are very specific. They pinpoint why prospects have not bought a product or service they know about and intend to buy. They then define the exact behavior that will overcome this inertia.

Pendaflex, the maker of hanging folders, created a portfolio of promotion programs, each with its own specific purpose. The company recognized that the decision maker for its product is usually an office manager or administrative assistant, a person with numerous tasks and priorities, and the selection of hanging folders is usually far down the list.

Pendaflex created a sweepstakes with a trip to Hollywood as first prize. This provided the extrinsic motivator to act now. A television advertisement supported the promotion and appealed to office managers' desire for respect and appreciation. The advertisement showed a male executive desperately seeking "Susan," the office manager who had gone to Hollywood after she won the sweepstakes. By appealing to a specific target audience with a specific set of integrated programs, Pendaflex created motivation in a product category that is almost generic.

Use Tricks of the Trade

As you develop motivational programs for your product or service, begin with internal ideation sessions that describe your targets. Firmographics—the size of your typical target, industry concentrations, the department, and even the title of your decision maker—are a good place to start. But the session also should yield a collage, a multidimensional picture of your target. There should be one collage per target segment. The idea session can then generate possible programs to appeal to various aspects of each collage.

Next, select and refine the promotion by bringing together groups of target customers. If your company's decision makers are conservative, you can add quantitative research or even a market trial to be absolutely sure the promotion will pay off. At the end of this chapter, Appendix 5A lists motivation programs, and Appendix 5B presents promotion techniques. Appendix 5C gives details on the timing and cost of various alternatives.

Casting for Bigger Fish

In many business-to-business situations, you need to motivate a hard-to-reach target group: high-level decision makers at key companies. What can a company offer these individuals that they cannot purchase for themselves? The chief executive officer of a highly successful Internet company in California described one "promotion" he experienced from the customer's point of view. We will call him Mr. X. His story is instructive.

The business-to-business seller was Ernst & Young, and the service was general management consulting. Several competitors offer a similar service at roughly the same price and have a similar reputation among clients. The Ernst & Young goal was to establish a personal relationship that will incline chief executive officers in its favor. The technique chosen was an off-site conference.

An important point is that only top executives of successful and large companies were invited, which assured they would be among peers. Before the conference, Mr. X was visited by an Ernst & Young partner, who asked him for the names of several people he would like to see invited to the conference as well. Mr. X did not have to say why he wanted to meet these people—perhaps they were experts in a field that interested him or were contacts he wanted to make to further his business. The reasons were not important, but the names were.

When the group convened several months later—at a luxurious and exclusive location—all the people Mr. X had listed were there. In the course of the weekend, he found himself in small-group social situations with each of the people on his wish list, so he had an opportunity to get to know each personally. There were many opportunities for participants to talk with one another, in both structured and unstructured situations. The only reservation Mr. X expressed concerned the formal presentations by the Ernst & Young partners, which he found less compelling than the other parts of the program.

This story points to four basic requirements for events aimed at high-level targets:

■ Exclusivity. In a quasi-social setting, people at the top do not want to mix with lower echelons.
■ Top quality. From meals, to rooms, to the reputation and expertise of speakers, everything should be the best.
■ Peer interaction. A major drawing card is the opportunity to talk with respected peers. Expert speakers have an appeal, especially if presentations are lively, but sharing with peers often has even greater appeal.

■ Respect for time. Busy executives resent wasted effort. Scheduling, access to the site, and so forth should be efficient, and participation should be worth the time invested.

BARRIERS ARE NOT ALWAYS OBVIOUS

It should be easy to figure out what holds buyers back, what prevents them from purchasing your product. Business-to-business companies often come up with plausible ideas: price, service mistakes, billing errors. Be careful not to oversimplify, overlook, or misread. Here is a list of some lurking demotivators that companies have discovered in Step Four.

■ Inertia: There is no compelling reason to make a decision, so it is easier not to make any commitment.

■ Overload: The buyer is too busy with other issues to consider the purchase.

■ Insufficient value: The benefits are nice, but when the budget must be cut, this expenditure goes.

■ No need: The features do not match up with what the buyer wants.

■ Delay advisable: The buyer thinks he or she can do better by postponing the purchase, because of anticipated improvements or price reductions.

■ Inadequate knowledge: The buyer does not believe that he or she has enough information to make a good decision.

■ Insufficient know-how: The buyer does not believe his or her company will be capable of using the product to achieve the desired benefits.

■ No money: The funds are not available right now to make this purchase.

Each of these barriers calls for a different approach by the seller. The task of the strategic marketer is to spearhead solutions to these demotivation problems, but only after making sure the correct problem has been identified.

PROMOTIONS INCREASE AWARENESS AND STRETCH THE BUDGET

At one time, the conventional marketing wisdom was that awareness-building and motivation are completely separate. The job of advertising was to communicate brand name and benefits, and the job of promotion was to move customers to act on the awareness that advertising built. This segregation of responsibilities was probably the result of organizational hierarchy. New brand assistants worked hard to come up with motivational promotions, and senior managers had the creative fun of advertising. The CLC perspective is that a great promotion not only builds awareness and brand equity but also motivates targets to take the desired action.

Promotions are so flexible that you can design them to address any of the steps in the CLC, depending on where you need to improve performance.

■ Motivation can be intimately connected with awareness. Use media campaigns to communicate the motivation program, or use motivation campaigns to raise awareness of the product or service at a trade show, for example.

■ Motivation can be tied closely to access. Channels can offer or participate in promotions. Furthermore, motivation programs may attract new channels or enhance existing relationships because they pull more sales.

■ A good motivation program is clearly tied to purchase. The whole point is to move targets to buy. In business-to-business marketing, the sales force often plays a key role in both motivation and purchase.

■ Motivators such as sampling or demonstrations can help customers learn how to use the product or service and experience value.

■ Some motivation campaigns encourage purchase now and in the future, which can create loyal customers.

In many respects, motivation is the cornerstone of the CLC because it facilitates customer learning. It is also a major connection between sales and marketing, which traditionally tend to be separated; that is, marketing dominates the awareness and access steps, whereas sales has responsibility for purchase, learning to use, and experiencing value.

Effective ways to motivate customers draw on two basic principles of the CLC: What matters most goes on in the mind of your customers, and marketing must always play a leadership role in gathering knowledge about customers in order to develop plans that move them from need to loyalty.

EVALUATING PROMOTIONS

The ideas throughout this book can make you and your company exemplary marketers—if you put them into practice and systematically learn from your experience. The defining characteristic of a great marketing organization is that its people are always learning—about customers, about competitors, about which marketing programs work, and how and why they work. They subscribe to Buckminster Fuller's aphorism: "There's no such thing as failure, only experiments with unexpected outcomes."

Effectiveness Measures

Promotions must pay. One chief marketing officer requires that his product managers make the following calculation: Number of incremental units generated by the program × (revenue per unit – incremental cost per unit) – cost of the program = return on the marketing program. The trick, of course, is to estimate the incremental units generated by the promotion. If you have a reliable projection of the usual volume that accounts for seasonal variations, geography, and econometric factors, you can compare this figure to the projected units. Or you can set up a control group, a market that will not receive the promotion and is exactly like the group that will. For more details on testing promotion and motivation programs, see Exhibit 5-2.

It is not easy to determine the costs and benefits of any motivation program. Relevant questions include the following:

- Did the promotion cannibalize other offerings?
- Did the competitors' response affect results? Can the competitors afford to continue their response, or will a second implementation of the program do better?
- Did the promotion create customer expectations that will be hard to meet later? (Price promotion is the classic case in point, but even sampling, piggybacking, and so forth can create expensive expectations.)
- Did the promotion enhance the image of the product or service rather than cheapen or dilute it? Did the tone of the promotion fit with the overall message about this product or service?
- Were there hidden costs of the program, such as Web site enhancement, artwork for print materials, or postage costs? The little things may not be so little.
- Was there enough time to make this promotion effective and to evaluate the results? Most promotions require considerable time

to plan and implement, and the effects may not be immediately apparent.

Some motivation programs are inherently difficult to cost out. The Pendaflex promotion described previously is easy in terms of expenses for advertising development, media placement, sweepstakes prizes, administrative time, and so on. But how can Pendaflex determine exactly what sales would have been without the program?

Historical data are a good starting point, but if the company is running a major advertising campaign or increasing sales force activity at the same time, these may confound promotion results. In the Pendaflex case, if a competitor doubles its advertising budget and gives away a trip around the world, this will affect results.

To assess the effectiveness of any program, you need a careful model of projected sales that considers both history and "outside influences." You may be the only member of the marketing team who has the perspective to make sure all these factors are taken into account, both in planning the program and in evaluating it.

EXHIBIT 5-2
Testing Motivation Programs

1. Use a test for each motivation program; testing more than one program together can confuse results.
2. Isolate the effects of different pieces of a multifaceted program. For example, a program that uses sales incentives plus advertising to customers requires several tests: advertising only, sales promotion only, advertising plus sales promotion, and no program (control group).
3. Avoid as much contamination as possible. Keep test areas "clean" by not running ad hoc turf promotions during the test. Keep timing constant to minimize seasonal effects. Test areas with similar geography and representative demographics, psychographics, and firmographics. Keep executional details the same (same advertisements, same timing, same values, and so on). Control area should represent "business as usual."
4. Consider program variables that can affect results: spending levels, execution of different components, details of promotions (timing, incentive plans, value of offer), segmentation and customer details, and growth rates in the target population.
5. Do your homework. Choose isolatable and representative test areas. Understand the product's history in test and control areas, and isolate causal events by referring to that history.
6. Measure carefully. Isolate the timing correctly; for example, do not count a mid-month start as a whole month. Follow the test area for a few months afterward to determine whether the incentive cannibalized future sales.

Failure Is Instructive

Every time you run a motivation program, you learn. When it works, you learn how competitors react and how fast. You learn how customers respond. You learn one more way to make your target revenue. When the program does not work, you have the opportunity to learn just as much, perhaps more. You may learn that you need to improve execution or alter the program. You may learn that you overlooked some characteristic of your targets or competitors. In every case, if you are disciplined and honest about your evaluation, you will learn ways to make the promotion work the next time or how to develop a completely different kind of promotion.

For more on program evaluation, see Exhibit 5-3. Also, for a regular update on new promotions and evaluations of them by marketing experts, see the Resultrek Web site (www.resultrek.com).

Organizations that demand success and punish failure may appear successful, but they drive out the intellectual integrity essential to learning. And that sets them on a path of decline.

SUMMARY OF STEP FOUR: MOTIVATION

First, the initial step in motivating business-to-business customers is to determine who should be motivated. Who in the target company is the decision maker for your product?

Second, different decision makers require different kinds of motivation. Matching programs to these various target groups is a key to success.

EXHIBIT 5-3
Learning from Motivation Programs

These questions help determine whether a program worked and why:
1. Was this program a good investment? Did it pay off in terms of profits?
2. Was the program easy to understand? Was participation easy?
3. Was the incentive something the target wanted? Did the incentive match the target segment?
4. On which step(s) in the CLC did the program focus?
5. What was the program's objective (e.g., launch new product, encourage usage) and was it met?
6. To what degree did this program build the value of the product or service?
7. How can the program be improved?

Third, demotivators can be as important to consider as motivators. If you do not correctly identify barriers, even a great program will not work.

Fourth, after you pinpoint decision makers and learn what excites them, design a program that is based on intrinsic or extrinsic motivation. Intrinsic motivation is always preferable, but some products and services do not lend themselves to this approach.

Fifth, motivational programs can be expensive, and the results can be hard to pin down. Evaluate any program against a baseline—what would have happened to this business without the program—to determine its value and true cost.

Sixth, motivation can be viewed as a cornerstone of the CLC because it moves prospects from the most basic requirements of purchase (need, awareness, access) to the payoffs (purchase, learning how to use, experiencing value, and loyalty).

Finally, motivational programs are a main source of continuous learning, but only if you embrace the philosophy that anything worth doing is worth doing badly.

Notes

Alfie Kohn has written several interesting books that provide unconventional perspectives on motivation, both in business settings and beyond. His book, *Punished by Rewards: The Trouble with Gold Stars, Incentive Plans, A's, Praise and Other Bribes* (Houghton Mifflin, 1999) is the most recent. His earlier book, *No Contest: The Case Against Competition* (Houghton Mifflin, 1992) is a provocative precursor.

APPENDIX 5A
Sample Motivation Programs

Situation	Examples
An introductory product	■ A free trial offer ■ Contests that educate and reinforce the product's value positioning ■ Problem analysis devices to help business customers understand their needs and opportunities ■ Money-back guarantee

APPENDIX 5A
Continued

Situation	Examples

A mature product in a competitive situation	■ Promotions to increase loyalty
	  –MCI's Friends & Family
	■ Promotions to encourage continuity of purchase or usage
	  –Frequent-flyer programs
	  –Thirteenth month of long-distance usage free
	■ Promotions to preempt competitive purchases by loading the customer's pantry
	  –Sign up for cellular service, get 500 minutes free
	  –200 minutes now, 300 minutes next year
	  –Discounts for long-term contracts
	  –Cash card for pay phones
	  –Multiple product usage combines for volume discounts

Get customers to sell for you	■ Business referrals ■ MCI's Friends & Family is perhaps the most successful sell-a-friend promotion in telecommunication history ■ Continental Airlines' second passenger flies at half price
Smooth out demand	■ Reduced weekend rates at hotels ■ Seasonal travel specials ■ Off-peak pricing for hotel and university markets
Make customers come to the product	■ Look for a computer with Intel Inside ■ Sign up for a prize drawing at a trade show booth
Enhance company image by affiliating with causes	■ Sign up for voice messaging, and we will donate free telephones to disadvantaged families ■ Sponsorship of charities ■ 5% of purchase price goes to a designated cause
Sales force incentives	■ Sales contests (trips, bonus, gifts) ■ Promotions that encourage aggressive selling behavior

Trigger channel or trade to act on your behalf	■ Cooperative advertising
	  –Channel partner shares cost
	  –Share trade show booth with strategic partner
	■ Cross-promotions
	  –System integrators offer specialized services for strategic partner products

Encourage usage	■ Voice and data usage combine for volume discount ■ Free consultative services for customer at a certain usage level ■ Frequent-flyer programs

APPENDIX 5B
Sales Promotion Techniques

Tools	Pros	Cons	Key Objective
Free samples/ service trials	Customers experience good products	Expensive Product must meet customer expectations	Trial
Price incentives –Waivers –Coupons –Rebates –Dealer incentives	Generate trial Encourage brand switching Stimulate dealer promotion	Customers are trained to wait for incentives Easy for competition to copy	Trial; continuity; preemptive loading
Cross-promotion	Introduce new product with purchase of old product	Sometimes difficult to coordinate	Trial
Contests/sweep-stakes	Create excitement Customer involvement Open display opportunities	Legal red tape	Trial; reinforce continuity
Trade shows	Demonstrate products to trade Sell on site Get buyer feedback	Time consuming	Continuity
Cooperative promotions –Manufacturer pays for all or part of dealer's advertisement –Two or more products from one company combine advertising efforts	Lower cost for both dealer and manufacturer Increased exposure for dealer and manufacturer Synergy among related products Coordinated message Reduced cost for participating products	Sometimes difficult to coordinate Products must share the exposure	Trial
Premiums –Free or discounted merchandise tied to product trial or purchase	Can generate immediate sale Encourage switching	Does not necessarily create loyalty Delivery of premium can be expensive	Trial; continuity

APPENDIX 5B
Continued

Tools	Pros	Cons	Key Objective
Point of Purchase –Banner –Mobiles –Take-one	Promote impulse purchases Educate the customer Create the feeling of sale or special event	Dependent on store personnel maintaining signage and displays Display clutter weakens image	Trial; continuity; preemptive loading
Advertising specialties –Calculators, coffee mugs, and other gifts with company logo, –Telephone number used as an advertising medium	Durable; the message is long-lived Repeat exposure	Supplemental medium only	Trial; continuity

APPENDIX 5C
Timing and Cost Considerations

One business-to-business marketing department issued the following guidelines for timing and cost of commonly used motivations. The prices are for the 2000–2001 period.

Motivation	Advance Time Needed	Estimated Production Time	Price Range
Sales incentive campaign	1–4 months	5–10 weeks	$200,000–$250,000
Internet home page	2 months	2 months	$10,000
Direct mail campaign	2–3 months	2–4 months	$.50–$1.00/piece
Bill inserts	2–8 months	1–2 months	$.02–$.04/piece
Focus group	1–2 months	1–2 months	$20,000
Customer education, end-user information	1–3 months	1–15 weeks	$.50–$1.00/piece
Outbound telemarketing (vendor)	1–2 months	Length of campaign	$30/hour/rep + project management fee

APPENDIX 5C
Continued

Motivation	Advance Time Needed	Estimated Production Time	Price Range
Internal publications	—	—	—
Intranet home page	1 month	1 month	$10,000
Media advertising	—	—	—
Television Creative/ production Placement	3 months	2–4 months	$50,000+ $300,000+
Radio Creative/ production Placement	3 months	2–3 months	$8,000–$15,000 $100,000+
Newspaper Creative/ production Placement	2 months	1–2 months	$15,000–$30,000 $20,000/insertion
Magazine Creative/ production Placement	3 months	1–2 months	$35,000+ $100,000+
Billboards Creative/ production Placement	2 months	1–2 months	$30,000+ $15,000+
Public relations campaign	2 months	2–4 months	$10,000–$200,000

Notes: All media placement costs depend on market reach and frequency, which must be determined for each campaign.

Chapter 6

What Influences Purchase? Pricing and Selling Your Product or Service

Of all the steps in the Customer Learning Curve, purchase is the easiest to measure: A sale does or does not occur. Although companies may agonize about sales accounting and other factors that can significantly affect their bottom line, purchase itself is relatively straightforward from the strategic marketer's point of view.

Purchase is not so simple in terms of how it fits into the overall CLC because of the unique interface it creates between marketing and sales. In traditional organizations, the responsibilities of the marketing team often end with purchase. Customer service representatives or functional experts handle the subsequent steps to ensure that customers learn to use the product, experience value, and repurchase. In the CLC model, the strategic marketer must make sure that all these efforts are integrated, so that customers not only make the purchase but also move through the remaining steps of the CLC.

A purchase today, at any price, can set up a negative future. Perhaps the customer did not have time to learn about the product; when he gets to know its features better, it will not be satisfactory, or he will discover it is not what he needs. And if customers buy at a discounted price, they may be reluctant to repurchase when the price rises. Any or all of these possibilities can create barriers that marketing must overcome in later steps of the CLC.

Two marketing elements are central to Step Five of the CLC and must be performed correctly if all subsequent steps are to proceed smoothly. These elements are sales (educate, negotiate, persuade, and then ask for and take the order) and pricing (arguably the most strategic element of the marketing mix). It would be hard to find two activities that differ more than the left-brain reasoning used in price development and the right-brain relationship-building skills necessary for sales. Whole books are written on one topic and never mention the other. But from the CLC perspective, there is a strong link between the two: To bring about a purchase, you must align your sales forces approach with an attractive price.

When customers are aware of the product and its benefits, have access to it, and are motivated to consider buying it, they look at the price. With the right type of sales help, the sale is made. If there is a problem at any of these stages, marketing repair work must be done.

BUSINESS-TO-BUSINESS SALES THROUGH THE CLC LENS

A great business-to-business salesperson is a force of nature, someone who hits the sales target no matter what. Nothing the marketer can do helps or hinders very much. Just stand back, admire, and sign the commission checks. Great salespeople understand and use the CLC intuitively: They find prospects who need the product, learn which decision maker must be made aware of the product's benefits, identify and overcome access barriers, motivate, and orchestrate the purchase. Unfortunately, such stars are rare. If you have any, learn from them.

At the other end of the spectrum are the marginal salespeople. In many sales forces, the bottom 50%–60% accounts for less than 10% of sales volume. Some are new employees learning the ropes, and others are talented people who are learning that sales is not their strength. Marketing has the greatest effect on the group between the bottom and the top, the B+ salespeople who do a lot of things right, barely hit or barely miss their targets, and want all the help they can get. Exhibit 6-1 shows the relationship between sales volume and type of performer.

The Sales Force Cannot Do It All

As discussed earlier, the sales force—especially the B+ group—cannot do the whole job of moving the prospect along the

EXHIBIT 6-1
The Typical Relationship Between Sales Volume and Performance of Salespeople

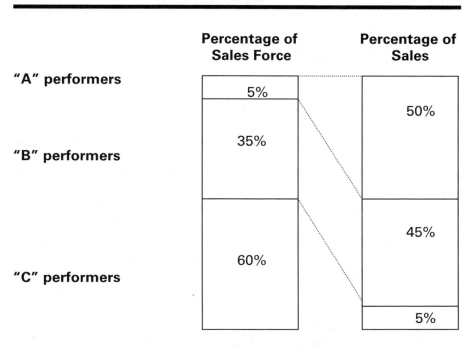

	Percentage of Sales Force	Percentage of Sales
"A" performers	5%	50%
"B" performers	35%	
"C" performers	60%	45%
		5%

CLC. The sales force is not the best marketing tool for overcoming many awareness barriers (e.g., branding), traditional channel barriers, competitive parity in products, prospect inertia, and many other problems. A central message of the CLC is that if you pinpoint specific barriers to purchase and design specific programs to help prospects over these barriers, all other marketing elements, including your sales force, become more effective. For example, it is easier to gain access to prospects who are already aware of product benefits and are motivated to engage in the sales process.

Although the sales force can often help make customers aware, give them access to your product, and motivate them to engage in the purchasing process, it typically is not the *ideal* marketing tool for these tasks. However, the sales force *is* the ideal marketing tool for orchestrating and closing the sale—that is, helping prospects over the *purchase* barrier. This is the sales force's job. And you can help them be better at it by telling them the answers to the three questions every sales person wants answered:

1. Whom do I visit?
2. What do I say and do?
3. How do I get paid?

Who to Visit

Step One of the CLC dictates the answer: Visit the prospect who needs the product. When you identify that prospect, do not keep it a secret. Profile your target so that salespeople can find them and discriminate between a good prospect and a waste of sales time.

As we described earlier, the Wholesale Industry Practice Area of a professional services firm went searching for the few hundred prospects eager for sophisticated management consulting among thousands of distribution companies. Discriminant analysis winnowed the 17,000 candidates in the Chicago market down to 300 that could appreciate the business advantage provided by this service. Previously, the firm's partners had a dismal time when they went out to sell. But when they focused on promising customers, they made presentations, got requests for proposals, and closed sales. Sales efficiency increased, and the partner teams had positive experiences.

BellSouth's customer service reps learned years ago that the best prospects for additional services were customers who said "yes" when asked whether they made a lot of business calls from home. Today, for example, these customers are automatic DSL prospects. You can help salespeople discriminate among prospects by giving them the qualifying questions to ask. Better still, do a survey for them and turn over a list of qualified prospects. Taking these steps will improve their ability to move prospects along Step Five of the CLC.

What to Say and Do

Much of the answer to this question comes from the positioning work done in Step Two of the CLC, developing awareness of benefits among potential customers. In addition, salespeople must be armed with different ways to deliver your positioning message to various types of prospects. A model created by consultants John

DeVincentis and Neil Rackham (1998) describes three different buying styles:

1. Transactional customers are "bottom-line buyers" who want to get the job done. They like to close the sale quickly at a good price. They do not want their time wasted and often perceive the offer of extra features or services as simply a way to add costs. These customers tend to respond to brief sales calls, telephone sales, or service through a Web site.
2. Consultative customers want help with their business and information on how your product or service can work for them. Send your best relationship builders and back them up with information and product or service experts. Give your team the time to understand the customer's business in depth, and be prepared to customize your product or service to the customer's needs and desires.
3. Enterprise customers want to form partnerships that can solve their problems. They may want to have input into product or service development, or they may require that your manufacturing facilities be near their operations; the needs vary but go deep. Salespeople usually are not qualified to handle such arrangements, but they can identify these customers and notify your organization of the opportunity.

From the CLC point of view, these various styles present different kinds of barriers and require different approaches. You must develop programs and tools that respond to each style.

If you analyze why prospects are falling off your CLC at the purchase stage, you may rethink exactly what the sales force should be doing. For example, transactional customers prefer less contact, and e-communication or telemarketing may serve them well. Pfizer found that many physicians no longer want to wait for a detail person to call on them with information about a new drug. They visit Pfizer's Web page, or download objective studies that report on the drug's performance and compare it with other brands, or visit online chat groups that discuss experiences with the drug. Of course, not every business-to-business buyer will feel better served by alternatives to the personal sales call, but non-traditional selling approaches can be inexpensive and adaptable, and they can be used to supplement sales force efforts.

Consultative customers like contact. Many want vendors to supply the latest information and ideas, which they assimilate and use in making their decisions. Some even want the vendor to do all the work of developing the solution. Traditional sales training focuses on how to sell effectively and talk about features and benefits, but the education process must go farther if salespeople are going to implement a consultative selling strategy.

The star salespeople intuitively adapt to each of these variations, but the B+ salespeople will need help recognizing customers' alternative styles and finding resources and programs that promote purchase. To serve consultative customers who want information and ideas, the B+ salesperson needs the following kinds of knowledge:

- An understanding of the industry, company, and competition of both buyer and seller;
- A one-page summary of market research on a product or service, including both your company's point of view and points that may be helpful to customers;
- Data about competitors to supplement the fragmented and sometimes inaccurate "street" information salespeople typically receive;
- Notification of upcoming advertising and promotions as well as one-page summaries of past campaigns—how successful they were, how much they cost the company, and what marketing learned; and
- Pricing guidelines that reflect current costs and profit objectives, along with evidence of economic benefits of the product or service for customer costs and profits.

In dealing with consultative customers who want turnkey solutions, the B+ salesperson may need education in the following areas:

- The customer's market segmentation and the marketing benefits to the customer of your turnkey solution;
- The financial effects of your turnkey solution, including return on investment, internal rate of return, and implications for customer margins and overhead allocations;
- Strategic insight into competitive offerings and whether your solution gives customers an advantage over their own competition; and
- Computer technology to support sophisticated financial models and databases both on and for customers.

In the case of enterprise customers, who are interested in a learning partnership, the sales force can be assisted in several ways:

■ Prepare summary reports of your market research, or white papers, that can be given to prospects;

■ Establish cross-functional learning teams in your organization to focus on improving performance in specific areas, both for your company and customers;

■ Provide customers with information on how to contact learning team members;

■ Give customers access to the specific department in your organization that can offer relevant insights and solutions;

■ Develop a computerized database to track collaborative efforts; and

■ Organize executive-level meetings and agendas.

As marketing strategies become more complicated, salespeople must be kept informed. An especially effective training tool is success stories in which B+ salespeople are the heroes who move typical target prospects down the CLC. Another tool is a 20-minute tutorial that can be downloaded the night before a sales call. And on-site marketing training sessions are still the most effective way to explain a complex sales approach.

Sales forces often adopt a sales philosophy, such as that in Neil Rackham's *SPIN Selling* or Michael Bosworth's *Solution Selling* (see the "Notes" section at the end of this chapter). A sales philosophy provides the strategic marketer with a vehicle for communicating a product's "message" to the sales force in the form of "problems" to be solved for the customers (*SPIN Selling*) or solutions to be provided (*Solution Selling*).

Sales Force Compensation

More than any other aspect of business, sales are driven by goals and compensation. Traditionally, the focus is on rewarding volume, which is usually measured by number of units sold or dollar value. Yet in the changing world of strategic alliances, electronic data interchange, and maturing products, costs are more complex, and a reward for volume alone can lead the sales force to expend effort on unprofitable customers. Some additional dimensions of performance should be kept in mind.

Profitability

When you select targets in Step One of the CLC, you choose the most profitable prospects, and in Step Five you want the sales force to concentrate on these. A focus on how much profit your company makes on a given sale is a radical innovation for many salespeople, and management input is required to drive a fundamental change.

Salespeople must be given enough information to distinguish between profitable and unprofitable prospects and must be taught how to use that information. Top sellers who handle large accounts may already understand this idea, but the B+ salesperson may need help. Management needs to make the profit priority clear and should provide guidelines, tools, and examples to follow.

Share of Market

In mature markets, competition for share can be fierce and may be critical in holding volume and profits. If the mature product still accounts for a substantial part of the company's business, management may need to keep the sales force interested, especially if selling a hot new product diverts attention. Some compensation options for the mature product are rewards based on meeting product quotas or capturing "share of wallet" (the percentage of a customer's total spending on a product category), bounties on share taken from specific competitors, and celebrations or gifts for hard-won increases in market share.

Cross-Functional Success

Jack Welch, legendary former chief executive officer of General Electric, insisted on both good results and good behavior from his managers. For Welch, reaching a sales target was not enough; how the target was reached was also important. In many companies, "good behavior" for a sales group includes participating in cross-functional teams that work together through all stages of the CLC, from identifying prospects through building awareness, motivating interest, general selling, following up to ensure satisfaction, and even replacing products when technological breakthroughs warrant it.

Teamwork is often critical to total success through the entire CLC. If an assessment of cross-functional performance is added to evaluations of selling prowess, good behavior is given higher priority, and salespeople are drawn more deeply into cross-functional teams. Furthermore, by tying compensation directly to long-term customer satisfaction, your company makes clear how much it values a happy customer. ADP, which offers complete payroll outsourcing and other human resources services, does not pay its national sales force full commission until the new client signs off on the first successful payroll. This may take six weeks or more, depending on the complexity of the job.

Customer Results

A focus on what the customer needs in order to succeed can be a powerful spur to relationship-building. If customers believe their success is important to the salesperson sitting across from them, they feel a sense of partnership that contributes to both short-term purchases and long-term loyalty.

To help the sales force become aware of how your offering affects customer results, provide questions to probe the importance of the product or service in the customer's business, celebrate success stories and write up testimonials, create job tools and templates for calculating customer improvements, and encourage postsale assessments. All these awareness-building techniques orient the sales force toward helping customers improve their results.

Support Change

Customer Learning Curve analysis often identifies the need for a radical departure in the way a product is sold. When change is on the agenda, the sales force is like all other departments in your company: The initiative should start at the top and extend down through the organizational structure. The CLC supports sales force change in several unique ways. First, it provides a total marketing context for the sales effort. By understanding how customers move step by step from need to retention, salespeople see how their efforts fit into an integrated marketing approach and are much more effective in implementing changes.

Second, the CLC provides a framework for collecting and analyzing feedback on the effectiveness of all marketing programs, including sales. Salespeople can fine-tune their approaches, and there is less danger of discontinuing a correct sales practice that is being hamstrung by another part of the marketing mix, such as ineffective channels or advertising.

Third, the CLC supports learning rather than blame. It engenders the attitude that we are doing 90% of the job right, so we need to pinpoint and fix the other 10%.

Fourth, the CLC helps justify investments in the sales force. Training, education, restructuring, and new information systems to support sales are expensive. The CLC helps quantify the returns from increased marketing effectiveness.

In summary, for the sales force to move customers through the CLC in general and the purchase step in particular, the organization needs to be integrated and focused more than ever on the customer. It should use technology to support its work rather than erode relationships. It should define target customers and specific roles and objectives for the sales force. It should be interested in measurement, feedback, and learning.

BUSINESS-TO-BUSINESS PRICING THROUGH THE CLC LENS

Price determination is arguably the most strategic decision you make as you move customers through the CLC. All other activities, programs, and decisions create value for the customer. Price is the only element that captures some of that value for your company. Both high and low prices have advantages. An exceptionally high price communicates: "This is *some* product." An exceptionally low price communicates: "Buddy, you got a bargain." In a price-insensitive market, an exceptionally high price captures margin, which creates resources to fund programs in other steps of the CLC; an exceptionally low price also creates resources by increasing volume and spreading fixed marketing costs over more units sold. Finally, an exceptionally high price attracts competitors, and an exceptionally low price discourages them.

It also can be argued that price setting is the most tactical marketing decision. The first thing a new business-to-business salesperson learns is who to call in the company for special pricing approval to win a competitive deal. The daily, tactical pressures on pricing make it all the more important to establish a pricing strategy objectively, so that salespeople and channels can be price-active within parameters that guarantee profits for your company. Objective pricing requires a long strategic look at the five C's of pricing: customers, competitors, cost, control, and change.

Customers: How Price Sensitive Are They?

A theme throughout the CLC is market segmentation. Different customers need different benefits from your offering, they process information differently, they encounter different access barriers, and they are motivated by different incentives. Similarly, different customers have different price sensitivities.

You must select the benefits to offer and the prices to charge that maximize the profit from each group of customers that moves through the purchase step. Three techniques place pricing issues into a strategic marketing context: conjoint or choice-based market research; qualitative assessment of historical data and the way customers view your product; and analysis of your price band, or the range of prices customers are paying for your product.

Conjoint Analysis

Conjoint analysis and its cousin, choice-based market research, test reactions to alternative combinations of prices and benefits, including completely new features. Customers reveal their preferences and priorities by choosing among these packages. Conjoint analysis predicts with uncanny accuracy. You can project market share at various prices and learn which customers will choose which package. You also can determine which competitors will win or lose volume as a result of price changes. Exhibit 6-2 provides detail on this technique, and Exhibit 6-3 presents a simple case. (Intelliquest [1999] provides an interesting perspective and additional information on conjoint analysis.)

Conjoint analysis is particularly useful in CLC calibration and strategy development. It helps you not only choose the best price for products or services but also define the most effective strategy for many of the steps in the CLC.

EXHIBIT 6-2
The Nuts and Bolts of Conjoint Analysis

1. Conduct several focus groups on a product or service to determine the relevant dimensions and factors to examine further. These may include price, levels of a characteristic (such as computer processing speed), channels of distribution, brand name effect, value of add-ons and augmentations (such as service, installation, and consulting), and packaging (both of one item and of items together).
2. Develop "trade-off tables" that describe a whole series of product or service and price choices. Respondents fill out a limited number of these tables and report how likely they would be to buy in each of a series of "anchor" cases.
3. Obtain output in the form of a "price response model." This model shows market share and revenue effects of offering alternative "benefit bundles" at alternative prices to specific market segments. It reveals which customers are most receptive to each alternative offering and which competitors will gain or lose business as a result. It also demonstrates what will happen if you take certain actions, either initially or in response to competitors.
4. Consider likely competitor responses. For example, if Competitor A has a history of matching and bettering prices, ask if this will be the response. If so, what are the costs and benefits to you now? What would you do next? If you match them, will they cut prices again?

Steps in the CLC	How conjoint analysis can help
Need	–Benefit segmentation: identify what each group values and what it will pay
Access	–Reveal channel preferences for each benefit segment
Aware	–Message design: What customers value and what aspects of your product appeal to them
Motivate	–Customer values from which to borrow interest
Purchase	–Price elasticity and utility of alternative sales approaches
Know-How	–Utility of customer education
Experience value	–Current levels of satisfaction and utilities of alternative features and services
Retain	–Current levels of loyalty and values from which to borrow interest

Conjoint analysis permits you to translate an understanding of the value you are creating for your customers into practical pricing strategies. (For a discussion of the role that value plays in pricing strategy, see the "Notes" section at the end of this chapter.)

Qualitative Research

Less rigorous than conjoint analysis is price-sensitivity research that is based on historical data. Past information about pricing changes—both yours and those of competitors—can be correlated with customer responses to these changes. The major challenge is that complete data are almost never available, which is why this approach is classified as qualitative. Nevertheless, past patterns can give a seasoned marketing strategist ideas about price sensitivity.

Another type of qualitative research involves customer-related questions, such as those in Exhibit 6-4. These require you to analyze a transaction from the customer's perspective, and the answers point to opportunities for price buffering or even price hikes that will not erode your customer base or market position.

Price-Band Analysis

Every product or service may have a whole set of different prices: a list, wholesale, retail, and online price; a discount for volume and early payment; a promotional or introductory price; a package price; or a no-frills price—the number of terms indicates just how widely the price a customer pays can vary.

When you develop an idea of price sensitivity among various groups, you need to know the price band or range in which customers are now operating. Now think creatively about how to manage price more effectively: Moderate or eliminate discounts for groups that would buy otherwise, or charge for value-added services such as shipping or special handling except among the niche of customers for whom this is a crucial issue. It is illegal to charge a different price to two customers in identical situations, but there is often a critical distinction that legitimizes a price difference.

EXHIBIT 6-3
A Conjoint Analysis Case: Assessing Ice Cream Options

Our company manufactures ice cream, and we want to know the relationship between price sensitivity and flavor sensitivity for our customers. We offer this chart to research subjects and step them through which product they would buy first, second, and so on, until all the options are covered.

Here is the order of how one group of subjects chose among nine options:

Cost/Flavor	Vanilla	Chocolate	Licorice
$1	3	1	7
$2	4	2	8
$5	6	5	9

As this chart shows, price is not the only consideration in purchasing an ice cream cone. As the order of choice proves, several respondents would choose a $5 chocolate or vanilla cone over a $1 licorice cone. These respondents clearly like chocolate a lot and would even choose a $2 chocolate cone over a $1 vanilla cone.

Another group chose quite differently:

Cost/Flavor	Vanilla	Chocolate	Licorice
$1	1	2	7
$2	3	4	8
$5	5	6	9

As might be imagined, there were several common patterns of choice. Putting each respondent's order of choice into a conjoint analysis computer model yielded the utility of each flavor and price. Adding profiles of each respondent permitted describing not only how much market share would change but also what kinds of customers would be attracted by alternative offers.

To the general question of which is more important, price or flavor, the answer is "it depends." It depends on the customer's situation, values, and possible options.

Notes: Steven Whitelaw, a market research consultant based in San Francisco, Calif., developed this exhibit. He also provided most of the information on using conjoint analysis cited in this and other chapters in the book.

EXHIBIT 6-4
Customer-Related Pricing Questions

1. Are customers aware of substitutes for what you are selling? Customers who do not think they have options are price insensitive. They may not have the time to invest in developing a complete understanding of substitutes.
2. Can customers who think they have options make comparisons easily? If comparisons are difficult, customers may be relatively price insensitive. A simplified pricing structure, even if higher than competitors' prices, can be very attractive to overwhelmed customers. Also, bundled products and services can introduce so much complexity to decision making that customers remain loyal because they simply do not want to sort out comparative features.
3. Are things other than price more important to your customers? If so, customers are less price sensitive. Reliable quality, just-in-time delivery, or such support as installation, education, and warranties may matter more. Even in bid situations, you can use special features to put yourself in a class of one and overcome the price issue.
4. What are current customer expectations regarding price? If there is a reference price, and your product is below it, could you try raising prices? If your product is above it, are there special features and benefits you can cite to justify your price? Can you raise the expected price by repositioning or making minor product changes?
5. Are customers used to paying different prices for your product in different channels? If not, perhaps you can differentiate channels and maximize the price willingly paid in each. There may be opportunities to adjust prices upward in channels that offer more benefits to customers. Or you may have customers who would appreciate the opportunity to make their own trade-offs on price/channel alternatives.
6. Do you have a strong brand or other differentiating factor that can justify a price premium for your product? If not, it may be worthwhile to invest in building such strength: through advertising, improving the product, or carving out a new niche. If you charge a premium, it may not be the maximum customers are willing to pay.
7. What is the "loyalty factor" in your marketplace? Loyalty can come from a long history of product leadership, strong relationships between your sales force and decision makers, or simply the desire to avoid the trouble of switching. Loyalty can command a price premium. Are you charging this premium?

Notes: Some of these questions are suggested by Rao, Bergen, and Davis (2000).

Competitors: Who Are They, and What Are They Doing?

No analysis of the purchase step would be complete without examining the main destination of the prospects who do not buy from you: the competition. The most dangerous competitors are often those that at first glance would not be considered rivals. Encyclopaedia Britannica discovered this when its business was almost totally eroded by online providers. While Britannica was busy watching Grolier's, Microsoft was busy stealing customers (Evans and Wurster 2000).

When you lose a potential customer in Step Five, it is easy and politically expedient to blame price. But if that is not the reason, and you lower price to win sales, you needlessly squeeze margins. Sometimes, however, price is the problem. If you determined that is the case, here are some approaches for looking at competitors and developing an effective pricing strategy to win prospects.

What Is the Truth About Competitors?

Most companies are afraid of their competition. Almost every mature product has experienced competitive onslaughts, including price wars. Consequently, strategies are sometimes constrained by folk wisdom: "Firm A is always a tiger when it comes to pricing"; "Firm B completely ignores little guys, especially in the first quarter of the fiscal year." Folk wisdom can be accurate or inaccurate. A factual history of competitors' pricing moves and responses can correct erroneous ideas and open a wider set of pricing strategies. Even a general idea about magnitude of actual price responses is valuable. Is it more accurate to say that when we raised price, Competitor A "followed suit" or "ate our lunch"? A pricing history should include information on channel changes, product changes, and the whole range of other factors that can influence customers in the purchase stage.

Exhibit 6-5 lists some price questions to answer regarding each competitor. The answers lead to a strategic pricing profile that will enable you to predict more accurately a rival's future behavior.

How Strong Are Competitors?

The health of a company affects its ability to pursue a marketing strategy. Exhibit 6-6 lists some questions to help you understand the context in which a competitor considers and responds to price changes.

EXHIBIT 6-5
Pricing Questions About Competitors

1. When have competitors changed prices, and by how much?
2. What were we doing at that time? Did we play a role in their actions, perhaps as price leaders?
3. Why did they change prices when they did? Was the change industrywide? Were there product changes? Obsolescence? Overcapacity? Changes in the economy?
4. What prices were involved? List price? Discounts? Specials? Promotions?
5. In general, do competitors tend to lead on price changes or follow? If they follow, to whom do they respond?
6. How aggressive do competitors tend to be? Do they ever back off? If so, under what circumstances?
7. Do competitors change their pricing structure if their position in the marketplace changes? For example, if a company moves from the first position to second or third, does this affect its pricing strategy?

EXHIBIT 6-6
Questions to Ask About Competitors' Strength

1. How healthy is the company? Does it have the ability to absorb price cuts or volume reductions in this product line?
2. Is the company under any sort of unusual earnings pressure? Has its stock price dropped? Is it a candidate for acquisition or merger? Is it planning a public offering?
3. What is the likely cost structure for this company's version of the product? Has it made recent investments in the product—manufacturing, research and development, advertising? Is there an investment in channels as well as production? Can reverse engineering be used to help answer cost structure questions about the company's product?
4. What kind of manufacturing and labor capability does the company have for this product? Can it easily respond to changes in volume—up or down?
5. Is the company investing in technology and research and development? Is it likely to develop improved features, new products, or new ways of cutting costs?

How Should We React to a Price Cut?

If a competitor reduces prices, the best course is not to panic. Here are some specific approaches to help you turn this event into a marketing advantage. First, take your time. When pricing competition heats up, marketing is usually under tremendous pressure to respond quickly. But the competitor may be making a mistake that will have serious consequences for margins and brand equity. A delay of weeks or months is not a good idea, but take some time to determine how customers and other competitors react.

Second, think through multiple steps of the game. One advantage of taking some time is that you can model the likely outcomes of various options and perhaps avoid a downward price spiral from which it may take years to recover.

Third, get the sales force on board. Responses to competitive pricing pressures are more effective if salespeople know about a change in your approach.

Fourth, when the news of a competitor's price cut arrives, you will be thankful for that conjoint study you had the foresight to perform. Its measurements of each competitor's brand equity and its projections of price-cut effects in each segment are as valuable as its insight into customer price sensitivity. Those findings should be supplemented by asking some additional questions at this point.

■ Why did the competitor reduce price? To steal share permanently? To use temporarily idle capacity? The answer is a clue to price cut duration.

■ Can your customer relationships withstand the cut? Which customers are vulnerable?

■ What will happen to share and profit if you do not respond?

■ What will other competitors do?

Your first-choice response will always be to improve or augment your product to produce extra value that justifies your higher price. For example, BellSouth convinced customers to pay normal prices for a new service even when competitors offered a free comparable service. Details of the case are given in Exhibit 6-7.

Another option is to maintain price on your main brand and introduce a low-price "fighter" product or brand to flank your main line. This approach enables you to bring different groups of prospects through the purchase step at different price levels, which increases both volume and margin.

If all else fails, you may need to meet the price cut. In this case, it is essential to understand the third of the Five C's so that you know how far down in price you can go.

Costs: How Do Yours Behave?

In most companies, the cost of a product is a potpourri that ranges from highly variable factors to fixed costs, shared costs,

---

EXHIBIT 6-7
BellSouth Pricing of ISDN

During the late 1980s, BellSouth invested in ISDN, a sophisticated telecom offering, but could not convert the technology into benefit bundles that customers wanted. A decade later, Internet service providers found that ISDN was a cost-effective way to set up customer access nodes. Suddenly, the long-awaited demand for ISDN materialized, albeit at a fraction of the original hopes.

BellSouth charged customers for ISDN, but competitive access providers began offering it free to the Internet companies. Because of the telecommunications tariff codes, they could do this and still make money from the call completion revenues, that is, the traffic over the ISDN lines. BellSouth's response was to emphasize its value as a supplier. Customers received the following, for a price:

■ A bundle of value-added services,
■ Support from an account team,
■ Far more installers and switches available to meet future demand,
■ Technical expertise, and
■ A relationship already in place and proven.

The Internet providers by and large stayed with BellSouth and even increased their new ISDN orders at the normal price. They valued the total package so highly that they were willing to pay BellSouth for the same underlying technology that competitors were giving away.

and corporate overhead. Different costs have different implications for pricing strategy and for the range of options that will be profitable at all stages of the CLC. It is imperative that you understand cost behavior in order to make good decisions about pricing and about each of your CLC programs to reduce barriers.

Variable Costs

In many cases, variable cost decreases as volume increases. If this is your case, microeconomics suggests that you consider setting price below your initial variable cost. Theory says that this will drive up volume and drive down costs so that your price will be greater than your actual average cost. All your CLC programs will get a boost as the volume they build reduces unit costs and offsets marketing expenses.

In the case of services, however, the variable cost curve is sometimes the exact opposite. When service delivery is at full capacity, an attempt to produce yet more output overloads resources, and marginal costs increase exponentially. If the demand is temporary, the service provider can allocate limited output by increasing price or refusing less important customers. In this case, the CLC is inverted: Instead of helping as many customers as possible down the line, the marketing strategist selects the strategically most important customers. If the demand for service looks more permanent, the provider should invest in technology that makes existing resources more productive or simply in greater capacity.

Fixed or Lumpy Costs

Research and development costs and one-time investments can be truly fixed. Others, such as the cost of a warehouse or machine tool, are more lumpy than fixed; if volume doubles or triples, these costs may recur. How much fixed cost must be covered by each unit sold is a function of how many units will share this cost. In the short run, any price that exceeds variable costs contributes to covering fixed costs and is hard to turn down. But when you are running at full capacity, pricing must consider both variable costs and any lumpy costs that incremental volume may trigger. Once again, the CLC may be inverted, and you may need to select the strategically most important customer to serve. Alternatively, you may be able to justify additional lumpy costs if there is a long-term need for increased capacity.

Shared Costs

Call centers, a direct sale force, special pricing groups, brand advertising, computer systems, and the like typically benefit the entire product line. Although these costs are not "fixed," they do not vary directly with the volume of any one product. Beware of cutting products simply because they do not cover their "fair share" of common costs. If they are eliminated, these costs still remain, but total firm profits decline. The CLC can help you find the most efficient way to build volume and cover shared costs.

Time Costs

Some costs vary with time, irrespective of production volume. When a new consultant is hired, he or she must be paid salary and benefits every month, regardless of the billable hours that are accumulated. An airline must pay a monthly lease for a plane whether it is full or empty. When time costs are a major factor, revenue management is critical. The best example is different prices charged for seats on the same plane, based on models that predict which prices will maximize total revenue for a given trip.

During a recent downturn in business, a major consulting firm assigned personnel who had no billable work to other projects. Clients were told that their projects would be done for the original price but completed sooner. In this way, the firm created a marketing program aimed at increasing value and loyalty (Steps Seven and Eight of the CLC) and avoided eroding brand equity by discounting. An additional benefit was higher morale, since an idle consultant is not happy.

Cost Comparisons

Evaluate your costs relative to those of competitors. The low-cost producer has more pricing options. The high-cost producer must go back to Step One of the CLC and find a niche where the need for valued-added services can shift the battleground away from price.

Costs and Margins

Consider your product's life cycle. In the early stage, battles for market share may require prices below short-term marginal cost; you may attack three, four, or more of the CLC barriers simultaneously. During growth, demand is strong enough to sustain healthy margins; the CLC becomes a marketing optimization and tracking tool that gives you an early warning about barriers to address. Maturity is a period when you may be required to defend your position from competitors; the CLC identifies the most efficient ways to keep growth coming. Decline is a time for strategic choices—invest to dominate, milk by maintaining or even increasing margins, revitalize, or restage. As do all aspects of your strategy, the role of the CLC differs depending on which path is chosen.

Costs and Strategy

Set prices in the context of your product family strategy. You may want to price a product to encourage customers to migrate to another with higher margin. You can use the CLC to chose the most efficient programs across the product family. In all these decisions, cost is as important a factor as customer value and the competitive environment in setting price.

Control: You Have More than You Think

Business-to-business marketers often feel like price victims. Competitors cut price. Salespeople urge discounts. Financial planners insist that prices be raised to meet Wall Street's earnings expectations. A theme of the CLC is that you have more control than you may think. You can pinpoint the barriers your prospects are encountering and develop creative ways to overcome them.

Pricing strategies are a prime example of control. First, you can control which customers pay which price. Armed with conjoint analysis, you know what benefits each segment wants, at what price, so you can move each segment most effectively and profitably down its respective CLC. Second, you can set prices across product and service lines in a way that influences customers to migrate from a low-margin product to a high-margin offering. Third, you can use price to control the adoption of a new technology and manage the cannibalization of old technology. Fourth, if margins are not large enough to justify the marketing spending necessary to overcome CLC barriers, you may choose from several classic price-raising techniques (Weber 1986).

1. Raise price and perceived quality. Justify higher price with additional customer-valued benefits. In addition to making all sales more profitable, this may increase the number of prospects (Step One).
2. Sacrifice market share but maintain profitability. You will keep loyal customers but lose some of the less loyal, which increases

your margin percentage as well as your performance on the last three steps of the CLC (know-how, experience value, and retain customers).

3. Accompany price increases with communications that explain why they are being increased. This technique demands that you improve awareness of benefits as well as the profitability of sales.

4. Create new economy brands. Flank the more expensive product with an economy brand that has fewer benefits and a lower price. You will suffer some cannibalization, but total volume will increase.

5. Unbundle goods and services. Maintain price but remove or price separately one or more element of the original offer, such as delivery or installation.

6. Promote larger purchase lots, which ensures that shared and fixed costs are covered.

7. Reduce discounts. If your CLC analysis reveals that price is not the prime barrier, then reduce discounts and use the increased margin to help overcome the real barriers.

8. Make several smaller price increases rather than a single large one. Customers are often less sensitive to small price hikes over time than to one sharp increase.

9. Shrink the amount of product and maintain price. You need to go back to Step One of the CLC and determine how much of your product each prospect needs.

10. Substitute less expensive materials or ingredients. Analysis in Step One tells you whether fiberglass can deliver the same benefit as steel in your product, at lower cost.

11. Use less expensive materials in packaging to keep costs down. If customers are aware of the intrinsic benefits of your product, you may be able to cash in on some brand equity (Step Two).

12. Reduce or remove product features. In Step One you can determine whether some or even most of your customers need all the benefits designed into your product.

13. Reduce or remove product services, such as free installation or delivery or long warranties. This is a variation of Step One.

14. Limit the number of options and models offered.

15. Use escalator clauses that require customers to pay today's price and all or part of any inflationary increase.

16. Adopt delayed quotation pricing. The final price is not set until the product is finished or delivered. This is a way to free your product from aspects of customers' buying processes that should not influence their decision to purchase it.

Change: The Strategic Marketer's Imperative

Companies today seem to face virtually continuous change—in technology, competition, organization structure, and regulation. The expansive (yang) vision of opportunity and the practical, focused (yin) discipline of realizing potential are needed in Step Five to cope with the changing environment and adjust marketing strategy appropriately. Pricing is almost always involved.

Geoffrey Moore (1995) points out that at each stage of the product life cycle, the best strategy reverses the strategy of the previous stage. If you cut prices to build volume during introduction, for example, you should seriously consider raising prices to build margins during growth. Pricing issues vary at each stage in the product life cycle.

During introduction, the variable cost curve and the immanence of competition determine whether to skim (price high, to capture the premiums innovators place on your new technology) or penetrate (price low, to gain volume-cost advantages and preempt competition). You should also decide whether to accelerate awareness through high levels of promotion or try to keep the market for yourself with a low profile.

In the growth stage, if demand increases so rapidly that all competitors have all the business they can handle, you leave money on the table if you do not raise price. If you are fighting one or two rivals for the top rung, you may need to keep prices down in the short run. Also, it will be critical to understand which kinds of customers are most strategically important (from an analysis of who needs your product) and focus on capturing them.

At maturity, the main strategy is to fight commoditization by differentiating. If you succeed, you can maintain prices. Or you may need to retreat to the most loyal niches to keep prices relatively stable. If differentiation strategies fail, and niches are not large enough to satisfy corporate goals, you may need to drop prices to maintain volume.

During decline, if you choose to harvest, you will maintain prices and margins. If you choose to invest to dominate the aging business, you may cut prices to encourage customers to switch and competitors to exit. If you decide to revitalize the business, you may develop a migration pricing strategy to encourage customers to leave the old version of your offering and adopt the new version.

The decisions necessary to cope with change require that you know who sets price in your company. In one telecommunications company, for example, almost half the dollar volume of long-distance sales was filtered through a "special pricing" group. If your firm has such a group, the strategic pricing practices discussed in this chapter must be translated into pricing guidelines understood and practiced by everyone.

Bundling: A Win–Win Price Strategy

Bundling is not for everyone, but it can be an extremely effective tool for moving customers to purchase. It also may help motivate customers and create barriers to switching. Bundling can be very beneficial to your company because it reduces selling costs. Furthermore, bundles that build on your unique strengths create entry barriers for competitors and exit barriers for customers. In addition, bundles can buffer the effect of price. High-cost products can ride on the shoulders of low-cost products in the bundle.

Terry Yarbrough, an especially creative and successful marketer at BellSouth, explains: "In order to work, a bundle must offer three things: It must be simple. It must provide the customer with extra value. And it must give the customer choice." These criteria require you to match bundle options and prices with the target customer's needs.

Will bundling work for you? There are several ways to find out. First, float trial balloons by having the sales force present different packages to selected customers. Second, use customer panels or focus groups to learn what products and services are good combinations. For expensive products, the panel can be drawn from one company to create a special bundle just for them. Third, use quantitative research, such as conjoint analysis or intent-to-buy studies, to gauge responsiveness to different bundles. For more information on "soft research" including focus groups and consumer panels, see Edmunds (1999) and Sudman and Wansink (2001). By carefully constructing bundles, you may well find a buffer against price pressures and may enhance your competitive position.

SUMMARY OF STEP FIVE: PURCHASE

Bringing about purchase demands a strategic combination of sales and pricing. Marketing and management support for the sales force can improve purchase dramatically. Remember the three issues important to salespeople: To whom do I talk? What do I say? and How do I get paid? Hone prospect lists, matching sales expertise to customer needs, and provide e-commerce tools. Compensation packages, analytical training, and better information on customers are also important.

Price can be vital to bringing about profitable purchase, and price determination may be easier than you think. Use market research to measure price sensitivity among customers and consider adjustments to enhance your sales volume and/or margins. Also, look carefully at competitors and their pricing strategy, historically and today. Then develop a strategy for reacting to a price cut and be prepared to stick to it. Be sure you know your own costs accurately. In addition to reviewing variable and fixed costs, consider other business components that may affect pricing.

Become proactive in setting prices. Your have more control than you may realize, especially if you think through pricing moves completely before you make them. You also must be flexible in responding to change in the business environment or product life cycle. Consider bundling, which is especially useful in extending the life of mature products.

Purchase is a challenging step in the CLC because it requires interaction among marketing, sales, and customer service. Measurement is easy: A sale is a sale. But to make sure purchasers move through the remainder of the CLC requires that all these players maintain a strategic, long-term perspective rather than succumbing to the pressure to make the sale now, no matter what.

Notes

Two books that describe fresh approaches for professional selling, especially in business-to-business settings, are worth investigating. The first is *SPIN Selling* by Neil Rackham (McGraw Hill Professional Publishing, 1998). The second is *Solution Selling: Creating Buyers in Difficult Selling Markets* by Michael T. Bosworth (McGraw Hill Professional Publishing, 1995).

Value as a component of pricing is discussed in *Business Market Management: Understanding, Creating and Delivering Value* by James C. Anderson and James A. Narus (Prentice Hall, 1998). This book focuses on value in industrial marketing, a subject that is not covered well in many discussions of price–value relationships.

Chapter 7

Who Learns How to Use Your Product or Service?

A busy and growing consulting firm purchased software to enable employees to transfer files to one another. After a year of frustration, hours of "expert" help, and many trips through multiple manuals, the software was ditched because it was too complicated. Another and more expensive package that promised to be easier to learn was purchased. Several months later, it also was abandoned, and the employees went back to sending e-mails or gathering at the coffee machine to exchange information. The two software companies lost a customer, and the consultants still had an unmet need. Why? Because both software companies faltered in Step Six of the Customer Learning Curve. They did not make sure that the consultants learned how to use their product, a significant investment from which the customer could not get value.

Although it seems inconceivable, companies work hard for their revenue and spend it on things from which they get only a fraction of the potential value. It happens every day. Brilliant market research collects dust on the shelf. Machines operate at minimal capacity. The zillion-megahertz computer does no more than word processing and e-mail. In the companies that sold these products, the chief executive officer trumpets customer satisfaction and puts churn reduction at the top of the strategic priority list, but customers cannot experience any value from purchases they never learn how to use.

Fortunately, not every company thwarts customer satisfaction. Intuit gains competitive advantage by helping purchasers learn how to use its tax planning and preparation software. Significantly, more than half the questions fielded by the company's help desk deal with accounting and tax questions, not just software-related issues. Instead of saying this is "not our job," Intuit staffs the help desk with experts who can answer both types of questions. They also participate in internal focus groups to help improve the next generation of products. Apple Computer is noted for user-friendly product design. 3M uses and shares its expertise as a powerful differentiator in its industrial chemical business, in part by encouraging customers to send plant engineers to 3M to become certified in using its products. This program creates not only know-how but also loyalty, because participants are less inclined to find out how competitors' products will perform.

PacBell, in contrast, found out what happens when a company sells a service without providing follow-through. To increase sales of its in-bound, toll-free (800 number) service, PacBell offered salespeople an incentive to sign up customers for six months. Sales rose, but then there was a high rate of nonrenewals. Market research found that customers thought the service sounded good, but many never quite figured out how to maximize their return from the service. When PacBell added training for every new customer, the renewal rate improved dramatically.

Customers need to know how to use your product or service. The more technologically innovative an offering, the more relevant is training. A large part of the marketing job is to educate, or to design the product or service to be so simple to use that it requires no education. Many companies turn the responsibility over to research and development, engineering, or even production teams, but marketers should be involved in all stages of thinking about how customers will learn to use a product or service. Otherwise, you are missing an opportunity to build sales, satisfaction, and loyalty, and you may create an almost insurmountable challenge as your offerings contend in an increasingly competitive marketplace.

EDUCATION AND THE PRODUCT LIFE CYCLE

Regardless of stage in the life cycle, customers need to know how to use a product or service, but the strategic marketing role of your training program changes. By matching your approach to the demands of particular cycles, you can enhance performance in Step Six of the CLC.

During introduction, the adventurous, curious experimenters who are often the first customers for a new product or service typically educate themselves. They may even teach the producer about improvements and defects. In the growth stage, marketers must find ways to build know-how. According to Everett Rogers (1983), most people need such knowledge to ensure purchase or continued use. Early adopters want to know not only how your product or service functions but also how they must organize their people and processes to obtain value from it.

As the product or service enters maturity, customer education can be a way to differentiate your offering from those of competitors. Business improvement training (BIT) refers to either classroom or computer-based instruction on how customers can benefit from an offering, such as better production or administrative processes, or increased revenues. A recent benchmarking study highlights the value of BIT. This study surveyed nine companies, eight of which market complex data or telecommunications services, computers, or industrial production process equipment. The results are as follows:

■ In one company, customers who received BIT bought 20% more products and generated 20% more profit.
■ A second company increased total profit by 5% and market share even more, in a declining market, by improving customer satisfaction and retention. BIT was one of the many factors that contributed to this remarkable outcome.
■ A third company organized its product training and BIT function into a unit with profit and loss responsibility. The new unit achieved the highest margins and return on investment in its division.

Each of these organizations understood their market segments' total product needs—including product attributes, complementary products, service augmentations, and BIT—and packaged and positioned bundles of know-how components to meet those requirements. The companies reported that their total solution bundles differentiated mature core products successfully.

Toward the end of the life cycle, knowledge of how your product or service works acts as a barrier to customer switching. The difficulty of learning how to use something else also is a barrier to late entrants. If your technology is proprietary and the next generation is backward compatible, use of a familiar know-how tool makes customers reluctant to switch.

Exhibit 7-1 shows the total flow of education throughout the product life cycle.

EXHIBIT 7-1
Education Needs Vary Throughout the Product Life Cycle

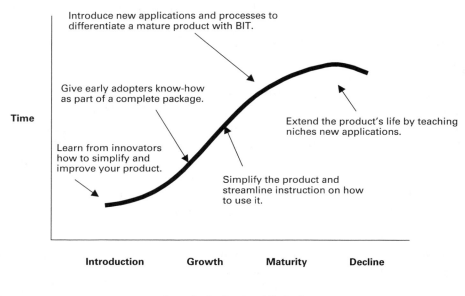

Introduce new applications and processes to differentiate a mature product with BIT.

Give early adopters know-how as part of a complete package.

Time

Learn from innovators how to simplify and improve your product.

Extend the product's life by teaching niches new applications.

Simplify the product and streamline instruction on how to use it.

Introduction   Growth   Maturity   Decline

Stage in the Product Life Cycle

KNOW-HOW CAN LOCK IN CUSTOMERS

Because time is a scarce resource, particularly in corporate settings, when it is invested in learning how to use your product or service, customers are reluctant to switch. Microsoft has been so successful with this approach that the government filed antitrust charges. If your company computers use Windows Millennium, Word for Windows, Excel, and Power Point, the purchasing department is not likely to buy computers preprogrammed with WordPerfect, Lotus 1-2-3, and generic presentation software. Inefficient QWERTY keyboards are a classic case of familiarity acting as a barrier to switching. No one wants to switch to the significantly superior Dvorak keyboard because it requires learning to type all over again.

Know-how also works to your advantage by creating loyal users. One public utility installed an enormous electric transformer for a major textile company, but a new technician flipped the wrong switch, and the equipment shut down. The company called the salesperson, who pulled together a crack engineering team and flew them to the customer. Within 15 minutes the generator was online, but the team stayed for two days to educate personnel about what could go wrong and how to deal with it. That kind of response builds customer loyalty.

It is important to keep in mind that perception can be as important as reality. This is particularly relevant in Step Six, because many people are intimidated by the prospect of learning how to use a new purchase and often are embarrassed to ask for help. For example, say the owner of an insurance agency needs a new office copier. He can call Xerox and Canon and ask to have sales reps call on him. They will come to his office at his convenience, talk to all future users, and evaluate needs and space limitations. The vendor selected will deliver the copier and conduct set-up and training. Or the owner can go to Office Depot and buy a copier. It does not come with technical support, but he reasons that very complicated copiers would not be sold at Office Depot.

At issue here is perception. Canon or Xerox would be happy to sell a simple copier to the insurance company, and Office Depot does not claim its merchandise is simpler than anyone else's. The point is that the peripherals of your product—where you sell it, how many dials it has, how you advertise it, even its color—send messages to users in Step Six of the CLC. An unusual case reported by Jay Klompmaker (1991), a marketing consultant and former marketing professor at the University of North Carolina, Chapel Hill, highlights the importance of matching appearances to customer needs.

A client asked Klompmaker to survey electrical engineers about their reaction to a simple, streamlined version of a highly technical measuring instrument. Many of the buttons, levers, and gauges on the old equipment had been eliminated because their function was replaced by internal computer chips and circuits. Klompmaker found that his subjects hated the new machine. "Obviously, this was made for idiots," one gray-haired senior engineer said. "There is absolutely nothing to do here. I could have my granddaughter run this machine—and she'd probably blow up the place." "I tried it out and it seemed to work okay," said another interviewee, "but I'm positive it would break down in a week or so. Look at it! There's nothing to tell you what's going on, and when something did go wrong, I'd have to call the company and wait a month for it to be replaced."

The new equipment was better than the old in terms of performance and reliability, but the engineers were not convinced. Klompmaker recommended that the client redesign the exterior to include some of the "bells and whistles" just removed. The revised prototype had a much better reception. Most of the subjects read the accompanying product literature, appreciated the new benefits offered, and expressed interest in purchasing the machine.

YET ANOTHER REASON FOR SEGMENTATION

If you have not already decided that segmentation is the recurring theme of marketing solutions, exploring this step of the CLC will convince you. Segmentation is a powerful tool for improving your company's performance in Step Six of the CLC. Consider the case just described. Assume that Klompmaker asked another group of engineers to evaluate the simplified machine and met with a different response. They view equipment with lots of arcane controls as inconvenient and difficult to use. The solution would be to design one machine with two different exteriors—one simple, one complex—to appeal to two customer segments. Here are some hints based on how actual companies have used customer education in segmented markets to build volume and profits.

Segment by How Much Customers Value Education

The school market is an important industry segment for electric utilities. Elementary, middle, and high schools often organize their buying decisions by districts that cover many schools in the same geographic area. Decision makers are often maintenance superintendents who have large budgets, especially for electricity, which is typically a low priority in the board of education's discretionary expenditures.

In one state that was an early deregulator of public utilities, a new entrant offered electricity at a discount in comparison to the incumbent utility, though other entrants offered lower prices. The new company invited school personnel to workshops on a wide range of maintenance best practices, including energy conservation. These were held in modestly upscale surroundings and targeted decision makers who were hungry for professional development. The sales of the new company rose.

Segment by Offering Special Services

A small company in northern California specializes in professional liability insurance for architects and engineers. It defends this fairly narrow niche against the attacks of larger insurance companies in several ways. First, because the firm understands the risks and the best practices for reducing them, it can charge lower rates. Second, it has long-standing relationships with many of the leading firms in this field. Third, and most important from the know-how perspective, it holds workshops that architects and engineers can attend to earn required professional credits.

These workshops perform several important strategic marketing tasks. They enhance the company's image of being an industry leader, committed to the architect and engineer market. They reinforce relationships with both the participants and their firms. The content and expertise presented in the workshops clearly augment and differentiate the company's product from the generic policies of large insurers.

In your product or service category, customers may not need or want professional training. But there may be other opportunities to offer segments of your customers special services related to know-how that can satisfy their unique needs.

Segment by Customized Learning

The distinction between literal and abstract thinkers is particularly relevant when prospects are considering whether to make a purchase. Abstract thinkers may quickly see how they will learn to use a product or service and experience value from it, but literal thinkers frequently require some persuasion, and it may be necessary to enlist someone in the organization to help.

Steven Whitlaw (2001), a market researcher in San Francisco, often encounters literal thinkers when he is selling market research services, which can be considered fairly abstract. In a presentation to the marketing vice president for a chain of hair salons, he made the proposal as concrete as possible. It outlined plans for internal interviews, qualitative external research with both current and new users, quantitative research to confirm findings, an analysis of findings, a working session with the client's marketing team to review results, support during a redefinition of strategy, and development of a marketing plan.

The marketing vice president looked through the proposal and asked: "So what are you going to give me for all this money?"

Whitelaw explained what he had already said in writing—the end product was a fact-based marketing strategy and plan. "But what will the strategy be?" the vice president asked plaintively. "I don't know yet," he replied. "That's why we do the research." The vice president shook her head: "I know your company has a good reputation, but I can't buy this if I don't know what I'm going to get!" She is a literal thinker if ever there was one. Whitelaw returned the next day with a disguised research report from another industry and the marketing plan that had built on the research. The vice president thumbed through the documents for about 30 seconds, gave a sigh of relief, and said: "Why didn't you say so in the first place? You've got the project."

At the other end of the continuum are the abstract thinkers. They pride themselves on being among the first in their company to grasp a new idea and enjoy learning about it. They can serve as innovators in beta tests and as targets of a marketing rollout plan. The metal fabrication industry provides a good example. A machine-tool company developed equipment that used laser technology to cut metal. When programmed, the machine made perfect cuts at precise sizes with no other labor than putting the sheets of steel in water to cool during cutting. Performance exceeded that of anything else in the market and operating costs would plummet. Literal-thinking factory managers were having none of it.

The company decided to find abstract thinkers in various industries that cut metal to precise specifications. They would buy the product because it was innovative. When these companies began using the machine, they obtained a cost advantage over competitors and passed some savings to their customers. Within months, the literal thinkers saw their margins begin to erode as they lowered prices in response. They quickly got the point and bought the same equipment.

A product roll-out targeted at abstract thinkers will be slow at first, but as the usefulness of your product or service is demonstrated, the literal thinkers will join in. At the beginning, you might position the offering as a solution to technical problems, then shift the focus to how it can increase customer profits or market penetration.

Match Your Know-How Strategy to Different Segments

There are myriad approaches for helping customers learn how to use your product or service: training to enhance their productivity, "plain English" manuals for complex offerings, help desks, online instructions, and inherently instructive product design. Each may appeal to a different segment of users.

Your attention to learning needs can build volume and revenue both by differentiating your company and by demonstrating your understanding of and support for customers. Carefully assess segments to determine the best approach, or even use approaches as the basis of segmentation.

ELECTRONIC TEACHING

Adobe's Web site (www.adobe.com) is a perfect example of how this medium can teach customers about the use of a technical product. The training is clear, is available around the clock, and is exactly what a potential user of PDF files needs to know—no more and no less.

Know-how training works easily in an electronic format, whether online or in CD-ROM or DVD formats. Indeed, many companies consider online learning their most cost-effective educational tool. Below are four suggestions for realizing the potential of electronic media for training.

1. Users want to have fun. Only a click stands between your student-customer and another online activity, so Web-based training must be engaging, intriguing, and enjoyable. Use interactive elements, such as a drag-and-drop exercise or a connect-the-dots quiz, as well as interesting graphics, colors, and motion.
2. Teaching must be immediately relevant. Most users expect speed and efficiency in their online interactions, so avoid erudite subtleties. The learner must know how the material will increase efficiency or effectiveness.
3. Keep technology simple. Users want to point, click, and learn. They become impatient with complex platform downloads. Applications must be automatic and fast. With the explosion in bandwidth, downloads will become less problematic. But until bandwidth is universal, you may need a stripped down version or a hybrid CD-ROM or DVD/Web approach to take the technology barrier out of the picture.

4. Users want interpersonal learning. The Internet enables unprecedented collaboration among students—through threaded discussion, homework bulletin boards, and multipoint e-mail. A community of customer-students is an invaluable marketing asset.

Do not choose electronic formats simply to save money (and remember that development can be costly) or to solve many problems at once. Your market has a huge variety of learners—individually, by segment, and by niche. Because their learning styles differ, you should carefully match your know-how approach to their specific needs.

SUMMARY OF STEP SIX: LEARNING HOW TO USE A PRODUCT OR SERVICE

Teaching customers about product use is an essential part of business-to-business marketing and is a vital step in the CLC. Customer satisfaction and retention depend on the value obtained from your offering, through both its functionally correct operation and its optimal contribution to the customer's processes and organization.

At each stage of the product life cycle, knowledge about use can play a different role in supporting the health of your product or service. It is critical for early adopters just after the introductory phase, for example, and mature products can achieve differentiation through business improvement training. When customers invest time in learning about use, a powerful barrier to switching is created. Also, perceptions about ease of use or technological sophistication are as important as the reality. Finally, electronic communication that is fun, relevant, technologically transparent, and interpersonal can result in marketing advantages for your company. These, in turn, will translate into better performance on the CLC and enhanced sales and profits.

Chapter 8

Do Your Customers Experience Value?

There are two aspects to Step Seven of the Customer Learning Curve. First, the customer must believe that the purchase delivered what was expected and must continue to feel satisfied during repeated use. Second, the customer must continue to believe that the benefits received are worth the price paid. At least three kinds of value experience may result from the interaction between satisfaction and price fairness: (1) The purchase is not entirely satisfactory, but the price is very good. For example, although a piece of equipment does not meet every need, the customer takes advantage of a closeout price just before a product redesign. (2) There is so little satisfaction that any price is too high, as in the case of an unreliable machine that affects the whole production process. (3) Even a premium price is a good value because the benefits received are so great. For example, costly equipment is installed free, lowers operating costs, and has a ten-year on-site warranty.

To determine whether your customers are experiencing value, you must measure both their satisfaction with a purchase and their assessment of whether the benefits received are worth the price paid. The customer satisfaction distribution shown in Exhibit 8-1 is typical. More than 90% of customers give at least a good rating, and most go even higher. Companies with a large percentage of dissatisfied customers do not succeed for long.

MAKE USE OF SATISFACTION RATINGS

Even if your latest study of customer satisfaction reveals encouraging numbers, resist the temptation to rest on your laurels. Steps can be taken to improve satisfaction among all groups. Exhibit 8-2 reproduces the previous exhibit and shows the four customer experiences that underlie the five ratings. In Group 1

EXHIBIT 8-1
A Typical Satisfaction Distribution

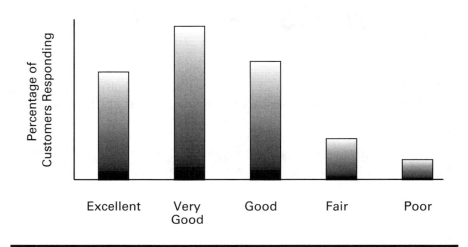

Question: How would you rate your
experience with our product or service?

are the customers you have delighted. They are so loyal that they
will gladly recommend you to others. In Group 2 are customers
who know you have done your best, and that satisfies them. For
Group 3 customers, your best is not good enough, and they want
something extra. In Group 4 are customers with whom you have
made mistakes.[1]

Let us start with the most obvious challenge: Group 4.
Customers do not give a rating of fair or poor unless there has
been a serious failure. To learn what went wrong, you can follow
the rating question with an open-ended item: Why did you rate
performance as fair or poor? Most companies then focus on eliminating these mistakes.

---

[1]An award-winning article on current perspectives on building customer
satisfaction is "Rediscovering Satisfaction" by Susan Fournier and David Glen
Mick in the October 1999 *Journal of Marketing*. The article, which won an
annual award as a significant contributor to marketing theory and thought,
describes aspects to consider in measuring satisfaction.

EXHIBIT 8-2
The Four Groups of Customers in Every Satisfaction Distribution

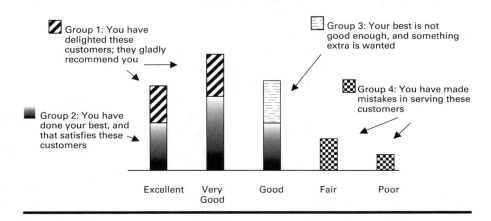

Group 3 customers give you faint praise for performing well enough, keeping most of your promises, and delivering much of what was expected. But something is missing in their experience, and often this is extra benefits. You may be able to identify these by asking a follow-up question on the satisfaction survey, but customers do not always know what more they would like. In-depth interviews with a sample of these customers may be necessary.

Developing insights into what customers want and how to satisfy them is a powerful way to improve your company's performance in Step Seven of the CLC and is a compelling topic in business-to-business circles these days. Many new approaches are evolving, and Johnson and Gustafsson (2000) describe one method for understanding satisfaction through what they call the "lens of the customer." The method begins by asking customers to describe what they like and dislike about the product or service being investigated. Then each specific comment, negative or positive, is explored. This open-ended interview format reveals what is important to them and identifies segments of customers who are looking for different experiences or benefits from your product or service. Similar approaches include ZMET and open-ended focus groups.

In Group 2 are the very good and excellent ratings, which for some reason are not unconditional. You need to find out why.

Finally, you should interview Group 1, your loyalists, to be sure you know what makes them so happy. This information not only helps you continue to please them but also may be useful for improving your performance with Groups 2 and 3.

Coca-Cola's Fountain Division, the business-to-business arm that sells to restaurants and food chains, used an in-depth approach to refine its customer satisfaction measurement system. David Kennedy, in charge of this division at the time, received one monthly number, a weighted average of a customer satisfaction scale similar to that in Exhibit 8-1. Month after month, the number was the equivalent of 3.8, with an occasional 3.7 or 3.9. No matter how effective and expensive a program the division mounted, the number did not appear to respond.

Kennedy began an in-depth exploration by asking the market research group to give him a distribution of the responses behind this number. After several months, changes in the basic categories emerged: An outstanding marketing support program might move more people into the "excellent" category one month, but a winter storm might delay deliveries and move more people into the "poor" category that month, canceling out the improvements.

Kennedy then requested interviews with different groups of customers as defined by type of business. He found that fast-food chains and independent restaurants assessed Coke's performance differently, new and long-time customers had different expectations, and customers who were price sensitive and insensitive did not experience value and satisfaction in the same way. He had the marketing team design programs specifically targeted at these various segments, and the rating eventually budged.

The important point is to understand the experiences of different customers so that you not only avoid the mistakes that alienate Group 4 but also improve the satisfaction of Groups 2 and 3.

SATISFACTION AND SEGMENTATION

Segment by Benefits

When you improve satisfaction ratings by giving each group of customers the exact set of extras they want, you are categorizing customers into segments that value a common set of benefits. This is somewhat different from thinking about customer segments in terms of the current level of satisfaction. Instead, the focus is on determining which benefits will provide the most satisfaction to each market segment. Exhibit 8-3 shows two different benefit segments (as opposed to satisfaction segments) for a high-tech product.

Determine the importance of various benefits to the survey respondents, and ask them to rate their current supplier—whether your company or a competitor—on each one. You will learn how to increase satisfaction among your own customers as well as opportunities for gaining share. Exhibit 8-4 identifies five different situations you may encounter when analyzing how important different product and service attributes are to your customers and how well you and your competitors are performing on each of the attributes. An analysis such as this provides a sense of strategy for moving key segments up the satisfaction scale.

Segment by Service Expectation

Various customers have different service needs and expectations. It is too expensive to set your service standards to meet the

EXHIBIT 8-3
Segmentation by Preference for Specific Benefits

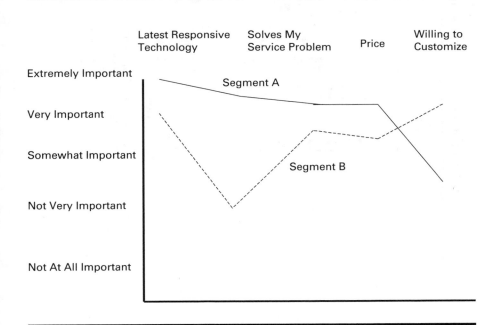

EXHIBIT 8-4
Benefit Segmentation: How Do You Rate Your Supplier on Service Performance?

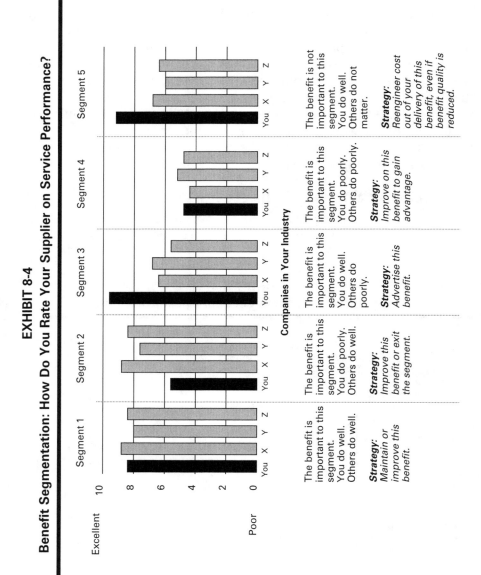

most demanding customer requirements of all segments for all customers. Consider, for example, the wasted investment in overnight delivery for those customers who do not value it.

Exhibit 8-5 graphs results from a study by a regional telephone company that segmented customers by service expectation. In the exhibit, customer requirements for speed of repair are compared to the actual time. The company used the research to change the approach of service representatives, who asked customers when they would like a repair completed and assigned commitment times accordingly. The company improved its "very good"/"excellent" ratings by ten percentage points, without increasing the number of employees or the total repair department budget.

Segment by Profitability of the Customer

Ellen Reid Smith (2000) advises that Web sites be designed for your best customers. She reasons that it is a waste of resources

EXHIBIT 8-5
Segmentation by Service Expectation

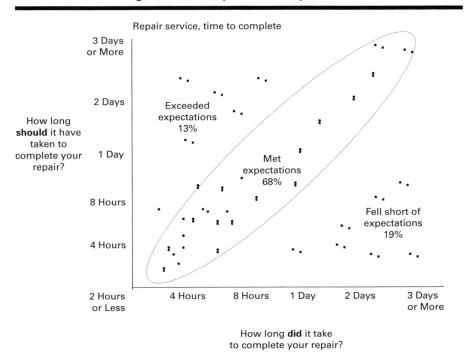

to accommodate the average or most common customers at the expense of the most profitable. Companies frequently confuse revenue with profits, but the distinction is important in all aspects of marketing strategy. For example, when MCI entered the long-distance market, AT&T fiercely defended its largest customers and even persuaded regulators to erect barriers around them. MCI realized that this left the very profitable "middle market" underserved. These customers individually did not generate large revenues, but as a group, they accounted for a substantial amount. MCI built its business by offering them small discounts and attentive service.

Smith (2000) presents a model for calculating customer lifetime value (CLV): Determine the profit from current transactions, project the profit from future transactions, and add a factor for the profit from referrals. This last component recognizes that some customers are as valuable for their status as opinion leaders and industry standard setters as they are for their own transactions.

OTHER MEASUREMENT CONSIDERATIONS

Whether you use a typical satisfaction survey or in-depth approaches, certain considerations should be kept in mind when measuring satisfaction. First, act on customer feedback. The only thing worse than not asking for feedback is to ask for it, get it, and ignore it. If customers offer advice and for some reason you cannot follow it, go back to them and explain why. Second, do not use customer feedback to punish employees. They will focus their attention on preventing feedback, not eliminating mistakes. Similarly, when employee pay is linked directly to customer satisfaction, employees are sometimes motivated to manipulate the ratings rather than improve customers' experiences. Use customer feedback not to punish or reward but to learn. Third, seek unconventional sources of learning. Here are several ways companies have gathered information on customers' experience of value.

■ Advertise for complaints. Ask customers to let you know when something goes wrong, and put your request right on the package. Set up both a toll-free 24-hour telephone system and an e-mail address to receive complaints. This not only gives customers the feeling that you are listening but also helps reach customers who may be unresponsive to other forms of market research.

■ Observe customers using your product, either in your facility or in theirs. You may discover problems and areas of dissatisfaction that would never surface in a survey.

■ Let the engineers and designers tell you what is wrong. Issues that were pushed aside during the development phase may still be relevant. Often these employees can suggest ways to fix problems that customers may not even be able to articulate.

■ Use ideation sessions. Several companies, such as Synectics and Eureka Institute, are known for a fresh approach to problem solving and to generating new product and service ideas. Look outside the box to change your perspective and thinking entirely. Both your own people and representative customers can participate. Use professional facilitators who specialize in unique approaches.

EMPLOYEES CONTRIBUTE TO CUSTOMER SATISFACTION

Exhibit 8-6 indicates that many factors are involved in the experience of value, or customer value added (CVA). In this section, we focus on Part 3, personal interactions, and the important role played by employees.

Berth Jonsson, head of SIFO Research & Consulting's international business unit, has worked with Swedbank since the late 1980s. One of the largest private banks in Scandinavia, Swedbank grew considerably through a number of acquisitions during the 1990s. In a report prepared in 1998, Jonsson describes his research findings about the relationship among employee satisfaction, customer satisfaction, and company profits, as follows:

> SIFO has monitored branch performance for Swedbank over the last ten years on three dimensions: customer satisfaction and perception of value, employee empowerment and attitude, and financial returns. Originally, we expected to see trade-offs. But instead we found that the three factors were highly correlated; that is, the branches that had high levels of customer satisfaction also had employees who felt that they were able to "do the right thing for the customer," and who were pleased with their positions and prospects at the bank. These branches also had higher than average financial performance.

Ten years of measurement created an exceptional wealth of longitudinal data that enabled Jonsson and SIFO colleagues to develop a model they call managing value potential (MVP). There are three major components:

1. CVA is a function of brand image, satisfaction with the product or service, and satisfaction with personal interactions. (Refer to Exhibit 8-6.)

EXHIBIT 8-6
Components of CVA

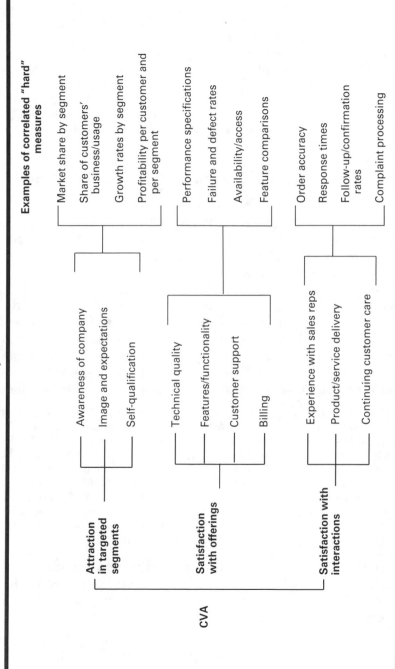

2. People valued added is the employees' contribution. It is a function of their empowerment, their ability to do the things customers want, job satisfaction, and organizational values, as shown in Exhibit 8-7. The six specific employee behaviors that came into play are listed in Exhibit 8-8.
3. Shareholder value added includes the usual measures: revenue, profit, stock price. How this component is enhanced by the other two is illustrated in Exhibit 8-9.

Swedbank's experience illustrates that the core of customers' experience of value is squarely in their satisfaction with the service's attributes and benefits. As another example, American Airlines has focused on its service's attributes and benefits. A few years ago, American removed seats from Coach Class (attribute) to offer customers more leg room (benefit). In response, United

EXHIBIT 8-7
Components of People Valued Added

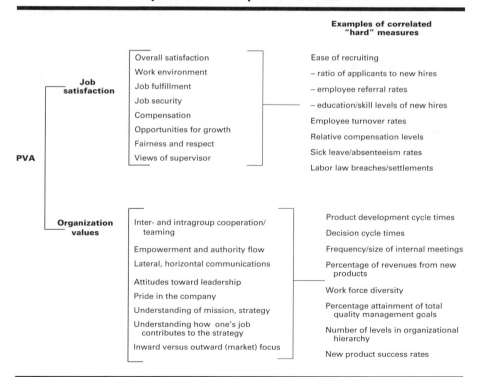

Notes: Reproduced by permission of SIFO Research & Consulting.

EXHIBIT 8-8

Six Employee Behaviors That Enhance Customer Satisfaction

■ Use judgment when relying on others to meet customer needs
■ Be resourceful when using systems
■ Trust customers with the full array of options when negotiating price
■ Be confident and armed with effective arguments
■ View selling to each customer as a unique challenge
■ Do not be preoccupied with administrative responsibilities

Notes: Reproduced by permission of SIFO Research & Consulting.

Airlines, American's major competitor, increased leg room on some rows of seats (but only passengers paying full fares could use those seats). American was already operating with lower load factors than some of the other airlines, which lessened the financial impact of removing seats, and it also needed to take a dramatic step to keep its competitive position. As industry analysts agreed, however, it was impossible to accurately predict the net impact on American's business because so many varied competitive responses were possible. Even if the reconfiguration does not last, American has differentiated itself by responding to customers and implementing what customers recommended by taking a benefit-oriented approach to satisfying them. The following are specific approaches to using attributes and benefits to increase customer satisfaction.

Pull All Your Employees into the Customer Satisfaction Loop

In the early 1990s, Volvo executives realized that intensifying international competition was a threat, though most employees considered the company successful. They were not told much about the customer's point of view because management only shared that information on a need-to-know basis. Despite good manufacturing performance, market research identified more than two thousand areas of customer concerns, ranging from gear-shift problems to loan financing.

Rather than assign blame and attempt piecemeal solutions, Volvo took an integrated approach. First, management let everyone in the company know what kind of challenges they were facing. Second, cross-functional teams were formed and charged with tackling various problems customers had identified. Finally, the compensation system was changed so that rewards were based on

EXHIBIT 8-9
Value-Creating Linkages in the MVP Model

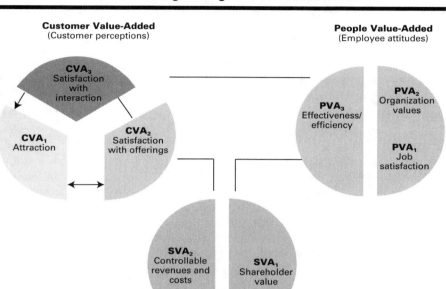

Customer Value-Added
(Customer perceptions)

People Value-Added
(Employee attitudes)

CVA₃
Satisfaction with interaction

CVA₁
Attraction

CVA₂
Satisfaction with offerings

PVA₂
Organization values

PVA₃
Effectiveness/ efficiency

PVA₁
Job satisfaction

SVA₂
Controllable revenues and costs

SVA₁
Shareholder value

Shareholder Value-Added
(The bottom line)

————— = Value-creating linkages.
Notes: Reproduced by permission of SIFO Research & Consulting.

both team success and fulfillment of corporate objectives (Johnson and Gustafsson 2000). The result was significant improvement in market performance as well as customer satisfaction.

The Volvo case illustrates an important point: All employees are ultimately responsible for customer satisfaction, and they must be aware of that and motivated to play their part.

Win Employees' Hearts as Well as Minds

In the heyday of dot-coms, start-ups were able to elicit employee creativity and extract peak performance day after day and night after night. Of course, some of the motivation was the chance to become a millionaire, but that alone cannot explain the devotion over an extended period. These companies addressed the emotional needs of employees, such as the need to have fun, feel creative, be part of a corporate family, and be appreciated. Some corporate policies even recognize the pressures of life outside the workplace, such as flex time for people with young children or aging parents, or concierge services that handle dry cleaning and similar errands.

Jon Katzenbach (2000) describes a systematic way to look at a company's history, values, and sources of energy in terms of how these attract and motivate employees. He summarizes "Five Paths" or corporate types.

1. *Mission, Values, and Pride.* Some organizations can tap a noble history and purpose or can be energized by charismatic leadership and "impossible dreams." Motivation emphasizes character, values of the organization, and the value of employee contributions. Examples are the Marine Corps and 3M.
2. *Process and Matrix.* Certain companies are oriented toward clarity, consistency, and information. They are energized by demanding customers in a demanding marketplace. Employees want a part in the leadership of the company, job satisfaction, and clear performance expectations. An example is Johnson Controls.
3. *Entrepreneurial Spirit.* This high-risk, high-reward environment is energized by a dynamic marketplace and magnetic leaders. Motivate employees with the chance to grow and excel, meaningful rewards, and acknowledgment of their contributions. Examples are BMC and Vail Ski School.
4. *Individual Achievement.* Organizations of this type engage ambitious employees who want to operate on the edge without risking personal security. They are energized by a demanding marketplace and demanding customers. Motivations include a clear understanding of what is important in the company, directions on how to perform well, and opportunities to be part of the organization. An example is McKinsey & Company.
5. *Recognition and Celebration.* Organizations in this category need "average" employees to perform well despite a nonstimulating environment. The energizers are strong leaders, a demanding marketplace, and a strong purpose. Motivation is based on tying individuals into the "collective energy" of the organization, showing them their value to the company, and rewarding them accordingly. An example is Southwest Airlines.

Identify the approach that best fits your organization in order to win whole-hearted support from employees.

Get the Attention of Employees and Keep It

Most people in organizations either do not read or forget much of the information they receive. Part of the problem is information overload. Davenport and Beck (2000) suggest several ways to help employees focus on what is important to the whole company, such as improving customer satisfaction. First, take advantage of all the media at your disposal: Send e-mails, memos, and videos, and hold conferences and meetings. If a message is important, use every means to get it heard. Second, keep messages simple and clear. Third, limit the number of tasks employees are given. Provide guidance about what is most important and should be addressed first. Fourth, demystify rumors. They will still circulate, but the truth can reduce how much attention these distractions receive. Finally, match communications to employee style. For example, voice mail messages to customer service reps who are on the telephone all day will not have much effect. For Gen X, send an e-mail with a URL address that leads in one click to a pithy, entertaining message about new customer service guidelines, training programs, and so forth. Marconi (2000) discusses generational differences and how each should be served.

Do not forget to listen to employees if they communicate back. When you get their attention, they are likely to have something to say. By acknowledging their feedback, you can create an internal loop that may greatly improve the service you provide to customers.

Help Employees Listen to Customers

Even an engaged, motivated, informed employee can use support in dealing with an unhappy customer. At a presentation attended by one of the authors in 1987, Xerox presented guidelines for employees. These are also helpful when dealing with your own employees.

- *Let the speaker vent.* Upset or angry people are not very rational. A customer who has not finished talking is unlikely to hear any solution offered, no matter how good it is.
- *Make sure you fully understand the problem.* "Engaged listening" is a term marriage counselors often use. Listen carefully, then briefly restate what you think you heard, so the customer has a chance to clarify.
- *Take some responsibility.* Even if the customer is at fault—perhaps failed to plug in the new die cast machine—find a way to

shoulder some blame: "I'm sorry that our installation people did not train your operators to check for that." Avoid an unsympathetic response: "That's not our problem."

■ If possible, *solve the problem right away.* Such a policy usually requires empowering employees.

■ *Compensate the customer.* Even small compensation may defuse a complaint and send the message that your company cares about customer satisfaction. If possible, find compensation that adds value to the purchase rather than focuses on price. Adding three free months of service may actually cost less than refunding the $500 purchase price of a service contract. By adding the time, you also avoid creating an expectation that your service contract will cost less in the future.

■ *Thank the complainer.* Dissatisfied customers go away mad—and spread the word. A complaint gives you a chance to keep a customer, provide information about your products and services, and generate good word of mouth. Let the customer know that you appreciate being told about the problem.

Keep Employees on Your Team

In some types of businesses, employees on the front line need to feel connected to the company and/or empowered to deal with dissatisfied customers. FedEx is an excellent example. Many employees are out on the road most of the day, interacting with customers and listening to complaints. FedEx ensures that every employee is given a simple job description and guidelines for each task, in other words, what is expected and how to make it happen. If something goes wrong, the employee is empowered to fix it within well-defined perimeters or knows exactly whom to call for a resolution. This referral is not viewed as passing the buck but as making use of the company network. And the person to whom the calls are passed always makes sure that the referring employees look good—both to maintain morale and to support the customer's regard for them.

Here are some ways to keep employees closely identified with the company, even in challenging times. (1) Treat employees right. Salary increases, training and education, and flexible benefits can mitigate the stress of constantly dealing with demanding customers, and happy employees provide better service. (2) Work with employees who work with customers. You are responsible for how well employees perform. "Dilbert seminars," for example, invite them to vent, just as they must allow customers to vent. This approach is especially valuable to personnel who listen to complaints all day long. (3) Teach employees to take the customer's point of view. NYNEX asked employees who deal with customers all the time to describe a situation in which they were the customer and experienced superior customer service. Supervisors and managers quickly came up with ideas for improving service, but many frontline people could not think of a single new one. Why? Because good service was not part of their personal experience. A few people on the front line mentioned Wal-Mart greeters. The point is that different employees need different types of support and training. You need to understand your employees in order to design programs to keep them engaged and motivated.

Consider the Upward Spiral

One school of management argues that happy employees make happy customers. This is the "more milk from contented cows" theory, and many of the suggestions we have presented take this approach. But Steven Whitelaw, a market research consultant based in California, believes that it works the other way: Happy customers create happy employees. This "upward spiral" of satisfaction begins with customers who feel good about your company and its offerings.

There is undoubtedly truth in both perspectives, and both have the same implications. If you measure satisfaction among your customers and employees and find that your company comes up short in either case, intervene as quickly as possible. Customers and employees ultimately operate as a whole, and improvement in one area but not the other will not yield good results.

SATISFACTION AND THE PRICE/VALUE EQUATION

Up to this point, we have focused on satisfaction, but you want your customers to experience value as well. Value brings price into the picture, though we have noted that satisfaction and price are not always of equal weight. Their relative importance depends on customer values, the competitive environment, and other factors. The strategic implication of this relationship is significant because you can improve the customer's experience of value by both moving satisfaction up the rating scale and manipulating the price.

The most straightforward tactic for changing the price/value equation is to reduce price. This can be done by offering a slightly older model or one without a few high-priced features. Another option is flanking, or creating a set of products that are differentiated by the features of each model. Customers then choose the price/value point that makes the most sense to them.

A flanking line of products also enables you to offer the same technology and equipment not only to different segments within an industry but also to different industries. A specialized industrial dryer, for example, could be internally configured in one way to make it attractive to small auto body shops and in another way for companies that specialize in repainting entire vehicles. Add internal racks, and the equipment might appeal to a large baking company for cooling loaves of bread quickly or to a small operation that dries organic fruit for sale to natural food stores.

Another way to add value to a product and keep the price constant or even increase it is to add services. Perhaps you have a strong service department that is underused because your product is so reliable, but you need it for emergencies. You might offer an extended warranty or routine service calls if research shows that these features are attractive to customers. The out-of-pocket cost to your company would be negligible, but the added benefit to customers could increase their level of satisfaction.

Any enhancement of the value experience is ultimately an economic decision. Focus on satisfying customers who provide profits to you, have problems that can actually be solved, and will become loyal to you if they experience value. Then make doubly sure that you fully understand what these customers want and need.

Bear in mind that costs arise from dissatisfaction, and these can at least roughly be quantified.

- Calls for expensive product support can increase, which adds to the workload of the sales force, help desks, tech support, and engineering.
- Customers are less likely to try to solve their own problems, which can be particularly expensive when customers have developed in-house expertise in maintenance, repair, and trouble-shooting.
- Customers are less receptive to product upgrades, auxiliary or related products, and cross-selling.
- Negative word of mouth can discourage potential customers.
- Customers are more receptive to the messages of your competitors.

In contrast, a satisfied customer offers several economic benefits to your company. There is less demand for support, and price sensitivity to other offerings is reduced. Cross-selling is easier, and positive word of mouth makes it easier and less expensive to reach new customers. Greater loyalty means less receptivity to competitors, and resellers are willing to push your products. The bottom line is that it costs less to maintain the customer base than to add to it.

In assessing your company's performance in Step Seven of the CLC, look at specific interventions for improving customer satisfaction and quantify the costs and benefits of each. For example, if it costs $50 for the average call to your help desk, it clearly would be desirable to process 1000 fewer calls per quarter. Determine how that can be achieved, that is, the problems that result in the greatest number of calls, and how much it will cost to address them.

THE ROLE OF E-COMMERCE IN VALUE AND SATISFACTION

The popular press often identifies sophisticated technology and computer-oriented business operations as the cause of dissatisfaction and reduced value experiences for customers. That view is not entirely inaccurate, as call-routing systems and overworked online help desks demonstrate, but technology and e-commerce also have a positive role to play. The secret is to keep the customer's experience in mind.

General Electric, originator of the highly successful and widely emulated Six Sigma system of quality improvement, believes that nothing can be taken for granted. GE not only has uncovered unexpected information about how and when customers like to use e-commerce but also has researched the nitty-gritty: how many mouse clicks customers are willing to make to obtain information, how fast they want sites to load, and exactly what information they feel comfortable using online today. The following approaches have been successful for GE and other companies.

Use Live Help to Support E-Communication

A major frustration for many customers who use e-commerce is the unavailability of human help when they encounter an intractable electronic problem. Even though business-to-business customers tend to be computer literate or even expert, glitches and delays can occur.

Quintus Corporation (2000), which is e-commerce oriented, points out that most companies see the value of providing self-help information and e-mail support to customers, but live help can play an important role in both competitive differentiation and customer satisfaction. Customers can save time (particularly valuable in business-to-business settings), ask complex questions and get direct answers, receive a favorable impression about service, and simply feel better about a human interaction. In summary, live support complements technology.

Use E-Communication to Enrich Messages

Simply adding basic e-communication to the other media you use may not be enough. One financial services firm uses worldwide satellite broadcasts and streaming video Webcasts (both with translations into foreign languages) to reach customers who otherwise may look only at Web pages and e-mails (Davenport and Beck 2000). Other business-to-business companies support customer chat rooms, video conferencing, and commuter-friendly audio cassettes about products and other general business topics.

Use E-Commerce to Satisfy Markets

Many business-to-business companies have built their primary offering around the Web: online auction sites, buying consortiums, and other forms of exchange. They are not just sellers to customer companies but central clearing houses.

One primary target market for Milacron, a company that sells machine tools, is small machine shops. Its Web site allows customers to buy and sell used equipment, provides a software "wizard" that helps them choose products from the Milacron line (replacing some sales visits), and offers advice and ideas on business opportunities for the small machine shop (Wise and Morrison 2000). Milacron thus gains a substantial competitive advantage and reaches a highly fragmented customer base that is expensive to access through a traditional sales force. At the same time, Milacron increases satisfaction and value among these customers.

Does E-Commerce Pay?

A study by the Center for Research in Electronic Commerce, University of Texas, found that when companies invest in e-commerce in the right areas and right ways, they improve their financial health: higher gross margins, revenue per employee, return on assets, and return on capital (Kirkpatrick 2000). Two aspects of these investments are noteworthy. First, certain electronic services had a high correlation between financial success for the company and customer satisfaction: (1) online payment, (2) electronic order modification, (3) electronic updates on order status, and (4) a secure Web site for financial transactions. Second, successful companies offered financial incentives to go online and solved problems for customers when they used online capabilities. For example, Dell's "Premier Pages" enable companies to configure which Dell systems their employees can order, which ensures consistency in both ordering and usage across the company.

SPECIAL VALUE CONSIDERATIONS FOR SERVICE BUSINESSES

Service companies are not in the same position as manufacturers in terms of customer satisfaction and the price/value relationship. A piece of equipment need only function well to provide ongoing satisfaction, but services are benefit "bundles" that are produced and consumed simultaneously. Joe Pine and Jim Gilmore (2000) propose that service businesses are like theater: Employees are performers, the place where service is delivered is the stage, and the goods delivered are props. And as any theatergoer can attest, the demands made on the actors—for high performance, ongoing engagement, and sheer entertainment—are great.

How can service businesses, or even businesses that must offer a high level of service support for products, deal with the demands of delivering satisfaction? Here are some approaches that have worked for successful service providers.

Train Well

Accenture not only provides clients with highly specialized services but also offers basic consulting services, the delivery of which can be broken down into routine components. The company hires hundreds of new MBAs and has developed a training program for these routine activities. New hires who complete the program can provide basic client services as effectively and efficiently as professionals with years of experience.

Define Customer Satisfaction

Many service providers subscribe to the "quality is free" philosophy because correct performance of a service is no more costly than poor performance. Doing it right the first time not only creates customer satisfaction but also saves the company the cost of repeating work. Companies have found that a clear definition of "correct service" is essential, and results are even better when employees are involved in creating the definition. Even before training in the necessary skills begins, employees are primed to think in terms of customer satisfaction.

Create and Support Unique Customer Expectations

The Ritz-Carlton chain prides itself on providing the most pampering service for hotel guests. It supports the expectation of luxury with top-drawer facilities, information systems that track customer preferences and experiences, employee training and empowerment, and excellent branding. Because the Ritz-Carlton experience is consistent and unique, customers perceive value despite high prices.

Educate Customers

The customer is a full participant in service delivery. Consequently, the smarter your customer, the greater is the potential for satisfaction. Just as an "educated customer" appreciates a fine meal at an elite restaurant, your customer must be educated to appreciate the full value of your consulting services, the complex utility of your new software package, or the cost savings that can be realized by subscribing to your online data information service.

Consider Strategic Alliances with Customers

Some business-to-business service providers find that strategic alliances rather than arm's-length supplier relationships increase customer satisfaction. Joint teams define customer needs, coordinate service provisions, and troubleshoot the delivery.

In summary, marketing strategists in service settings must be highly creative and willing to take risks. A low profile is appropriate for hibernation, not growth.

SUMMARY OF STEP SEVEN: EXPERIENCING VALUE AND SATISFACTION

Value and satisfaction are closely related but not the same, because value involves price. To measure both, you must fully understand your customers' perceptions and perspectives. One simple number or set of graphs can never capture this richness and complexity.

As in so many steps of the CLC, segmentation plays a role, especially in terms of customer perceptions of benefits. Employees also play a role in Step Seven. Employees are worth the investment in training and support to help ensure customer satisfaction.

To provide your customers with an experience of value, you must manage price, features, and services offered. In addition, e-commerce can have a powerful influence on satisfaction and value as well as sales and profits. With customer experiences and preferences in mind, you can use e-commerce as a positive force to support your business.

Chapter 9

Are You Creating Loyal Users?

Customer loyalty is valuable. According to James Heskitt and colleagues (1994), it costs up to eight times as much to win a new customer as to serve an existing customer. An increase in loyalty of 5% can raise profits by as much as 85%, and the lifetime value of loyalty is substantial: $332,000 for a Cadillac buyer and in the billions of dollars for a purchaser of commercial aircraft. That is why creating loyalty is a vital part of the Customer Learning Curve. Like satisfaction and the experience of value, however, loyalty is not a simple concept to define, much less measure, evaluate, and build.

What constitutes loyalty? Your customer care department says that 90% of current customers intend to purchase again from you. Do you have a 90% loyalty rate? Or a customer survey indicates that on a five-point satisfaction scale, your company scores 4.1. Should you assume that these satisfied customers are loyal? Or the last ten contracts your company closed were with new customers referred to you by old customers. Are those old customers loyal? The answers to these questions are not simple, partly because of the difference between intent and action. It is easy to make plans, but acting on them requires a strong degree of commitment.

Let us say a satisfied customer intends to purchase from you again. Various circumstances may arise to prevent that action. The customer may gather new information on the competition that makes other offerings more attractive, or the competition may approach the customer with better prices, new products, or enhanced services. Your company may change prices or offerings in a way that makes them less attractive. The customer may not have enough money for certain purchases, despite desire and intent. Your relationship with the customer may be eroded by dissatisfaction with product performance, poor service, or other problems.

SATISFACTION AND LOYALTY ARE NOT QUITE THE SAME

Satisfaction reflects a customer's experience at one point, whereas loyalty accumulates over time. Long-time customers may be willing to overlook occasional problems or mistakes because their overall experience is good, they have an investment in the relationship, and they feel they get good value for their money. In that way, loyalty influences satisfaction. In the reverse direction, a dissatisfied buyer is likely to look for alternatives, but satisfaction is not the only factor in loyalty.

Options matter. A satisfied customer with many choices is less likely to remain loyal than a satisfied customer with few choices. And dissatisfied customers who see no options are inclined to work with a supplier to get what they want because switching is not possible.

Telefonica had a telecommunications monopoly in Spain until the industry was opened to competition, whereupon the company conducted market research to identify which business-to-business customers were likely to switch to a new provider. Were customers truly loyal, or did they simply have no options in the past? Contrary to expectations, the largest and most sophisticated customers, many of whom had long been critical of Telefonica's service, were less likely to switch than smaller businesses. Why? Because the big companies had concluded that unproven suppliers might not perform as well. Telefonica was not perfect, but an unknown might be even worse. The companies preferred to work with Telefonica to eliminate problems.

Loyalty is fluid and fragile. If a loyal customer is prepared to make yet another purchase but your salesperson misses the meeting to close the deal, the relationship is jeopardized. Loyalty can never be taken for granted.

Some satisfied customers may want to be loyal but are prevented by law, as in the case of government contracts that must be bid annually. Identifying which customers can be loyal is covered later in this chapter.

MEASURING LOYALTY

How you define loyalty depends on what you are selling. If you market commercial jet planes to the airlines, repurchase of a certain airplane model may never occur; planes last a long time, and the industry is so volatile that replacement or fleet expansion can be delayed. If you sell steel to auto manufacturers, exactly the same product may be bought repeatedly for years. Here are some common definitions of loyalty:

■ *Repurchase*. This is relevant when a product changes very little or not at all.

■ *Frequency of repurchase*. How often a customer buys from you rather than the competition is important.

■ *Percentage of category purchase*. This is your unit or dollar volume relative to competitors'.

■ *Expansion of purchase*. Does the customer purchase other items or services from you in addition to what was bought in the past? This can include support for the original purchase (service contracts, parts and repairs) or completely new transactions (delivery vans after a purchase of cars for salespeople).

■ *Retention*. This is particularly important for time-limited contracts, such as annual cellular phone service or consulting services.

■ *Quality of relationships*. When purchases are infrequent because of the products' high dollar value and long useful life, loyalty is best indicated by the quality of the relationship with the currently inactive customer.

How you define loyalty affects how you measure it. Here are some examples of ways that both business-to-business and business-to-consumer companies have measured loyalty (Heskitt et al. 1994). Southwest Airlines asks frontline employees—at ticket purchase, baggage check, and boarding-pass access—to talk to customers and get an impression of how they view the company and of repurchase intentions. Xerox measures customer satisfaction frequently and in detail on a five-point scale. Customers who give a rating of 5 are six times more likely to repurchase than customers who rate Xerox 4. Taco Bell interviews 800,000 customers annually to determine their future purchase plans. These findings and others help project Taco Bell's "share of stomach." BancOne carefully measures retention of commercial and private customers and the number of different services each customer uses.

Different approaches work for different businesses, and your company needs to develop its own methods. The following guidelines may be helpful.

Ask the Right Questions

Xerox has found that satisfaction correlates strongly with repurchase, so it focuses time and money on satisfaction surveys.

In preparing the questionnaire, it is important to understand what makes customers loyal: product or service performance, price, product improvements, personalized service, positive experience in using the product, and so on. It can be tempting to include many items, but the questions should generate useful information. If not, you waste the respondent's time and risk investing in irrelevant improvements.

Decide What and How You Will Measure

The product manager of business long distance in a large telecommunications firm was called on the carpet one day because the customer care staff identified a monthly churn rate of 30% for this service. Business long distance was very competitive, and losing customers on a monthly basis was costing the company a fortune. What was he going to do about the problem? The product manager started digging and found that the data were faulty. If customers switched to another calling plan within the company, relocated from one sales region to another, or negotiated a different rate structure for their services, they were counted as defectors. The actual churn rate was not good—roughly 10% a month—but the original number was highly misleading.

The point of the story is simple. If you do not decide ahead of time what constitutes loyalty in your situation and how it will be measured, and if you do not have systems that can generate accurate numbers, you will not be able to determine loyalty or develop programs for improving it.

Gather Timely Information

Measuring churn, or the customers who are not loyal, should be an ongoing activity, and the results should be communicated quickly to marketing decision makers. A system that does not circulate findings for weeks or months is virtually useless. The longer customers stay "lost," the harder it is to win them back. Gross numbers and delayed reports prevent a quick response.

A large company that relies on service renewals, for example, calls within 24 hours every customer who cancels service. The cause often can be easily remedied: a small price adjustment, a quick visit by a technician, or a special add-on. The cost of calling these customers is more than offset by the value of retaining them, and the response often increases loyalty because it demonstrates that the company cares about them.

Focus on the Right Customers

It is important to decide whose loyalty you are going to measure. In the business-to-business world, where both reaching and serving customers can be expensive, not all customers are created equal. The top 20% often account for 80% of profits (Court et al. 1999). Your most profitable customers may be a specific niche or subset in the market, as MCI found when it pursued the mid-size accounts AT&T was ignoring.

A focus on a specific set of customers who offer the most profit potential and a deliberate decision not to pursue others might be called "preferential selection," a term coined by Steven Whitelaw, a market research consultant based in San Francisco, Calif. Exhibit 9-1 shows how preferential selection can affect sales and profits.

In an "adverse selection" situation, the customers choose the company, and these may be the proverbial "nightmare customers" every company hopes to avoid. The disastrous experience

EXHIBIT 9-1
The Influence of Preferential Selection on Sales and Profits

Three companies have equal market shares (33%) of customers, revenue, and profit, but
- Company 1's churn rate is 1.5% per month, or 18% per year;
- Company 2's churn rate is 2% per month, or 24% per year; and
- Company 3's churn rate is 2% per month, or 24% per year.

Over time, Company 1 wins customers from Companies 2 and 3.
- Each win for Company 1 is a "preferred" customer; that is, the account is 20% more profitable than the customers Company 1 loses.

	Company 1	Company 2	Company 3
Start:			
Share of Revenue	33%	33%	33%
Share of Profit	33%	33%	33%
After 5 years:			
Share of Revenue	38%	31%	31%
Share of Profit	42%	29%	29%

of a British cellular phone company, One-2-One, when it did not practice preferential selection is worth recounting. It demonstrates clearly the perils of adverse selection. One-2-One was a late entrant into cellular in Great Britain and took the easiest market position: low price. It set up three programs: Gold was directed primarily at businesses with high call volume and offered more minutes for a lower price per minute than did competitors, Silver was for smaller businesses and individuals with medium call volume, and Bronze offered a low monthly fee and free off-peak and weekend minutes for low-volume callers.

One-2-One thought Bronze customers would use cellular minutes that were not so attractive to the other two groups. They would make money for the company because the low subscriptions fee would be offset by volume. To promote Bronze and build the user base, One-2-One offered free calls anywhere in the world on Christmas Day. The promotion was far too successful. So many people signed up and made calls that the company incurred enormous expenses with overseas connectors—before the system crashed due to volume overload.

An investigation revealed that the Christmas offer itself was not the problem. Rather, so many marginal customers were attracted with the Bronze plan that One-2-One could not support Gold and Silver customers. The company began a painful process of shedding marginal customers and building loyalty among desirable segments, going so far as to change its logo and rework all its collateral material. Yes, Bronze customers had proved loyal, but that turned out to be a disadvantage.

A market can be segmented according to preferential selection. In Great Britain today, for example, Orange is positioned to attract young people who are heavy users of wireless service, a highly profitable segment. CellNet has a high performance position, aimed at the small or home office business user, also a profitable group. One-2-One still takes a low-price position and relies on free minutes and price promotions. Vodafone has no clear positioning as yet.

There are three steps for building loyalty through preferential selection.

1. Target preferred customers.
   - Define their profitability
   - Develop markers to identify them, such as usage history, credit rating, or past switching behavior

2. Create marketing mixes that discourage undesirable customers and attract preferred customers.
   ■ Conduct qualitative research (focus groups or in-depth interviews) with people in each category to understand their buying motivations and behavior
   ■ Develop marketing programs and select marketing channels suggested by the research
   ■ Test customer reaction to programs through focus groups or concept tests
3. Monitor results and make course corrections.
   ■ Find out which segments are attracted by each channel
   ■ Set up measurements of churn by channel
   ■ Find out which segments are attracted by each program
   ■ Analyze the "unexpected outcome" for marketing opportunities

Come Up with Hard Numbers

No measurement technique gives precise figures to use in Step Eight of the CLC. But if you first determine *what* to measure and take a consistent measurement approach, you can develop a set of reference points that enables you to both determine loyalty figures and plan for increasing loyalty successfully.

How to Build Loyalty

Ideas on loyalty-building continue to proliferate. All do not work in every situation, but the following suggestions reflect the best thinking in marketing today. If you integrate the ideas that best fit your business, you will be able to increase your company's performance on Step Eight of the CLC and raise sales and profits as a result.

Be Unique

Some products or services are unique because of technology, long-term market dominance, or position in the customer's mind, but this situation is rare and becoming rarer. Bundling, customization, and price packages are ways to create uniqueness in the eyes of target customers and help build loyalty.

Bundle Up

A bundle of features and benefits can make your offering unique, at least for a time. For example, AT&T was the first to combine a long-distance, calling card, and cellular plan, all for one per-minute rate anywhere in the United States. The ease of understanding the offering and simplified billing made the plan attractive. The company had technological strength in all three areas, whereas many competitors could only offer one or two of the products profitably at low prices.

In creating unique bundles, keep in mind that market research may not be much help. You are looking for something so unusual that customers may never have thought of it. Observational research of customer behavior may generate ideas, or internal ideation sessions.

Customize

Your sales force should delve deeply into what a preferred customer wants, such as the size of a piece of equipment, power output, operating efficiency, uptime performance, tie-ins with existing equipment, and triggers for automatic start-up. If you deliver exactly what the customer wants, you greatly increase the likelihood of loyalty to the product or service and to your company.

Package Prices

Many companies focus on selling a basic product or service and only consider "add-on" sales later. With careful research in advance, you can include components that are inherent loyalty-builders. Perhaps selling an electric generator with a five-year maintenance contract will ensure loyalty at least until the contract runs out, and this loyalty may extend to related products. The value of a customer's loyalty may be great enough to justify a free maintenance contract. Think through pricing in terms of loyalty value as well as income.

Segment with Loyalty in Mind

At every other step in the CLC, there are benefits from segmenting your market, and Step Eight is no exception. Loyalty can be generated differently among various groups of buyers, and three approaches are particularly useful.

Woo Profitable Segments

Avis "Preferred" customers do not need to fill out contracts or wait in line. A bus drops them off right at the rental car, which often waits with the engine running, the trunk open, and the heat or air-conditioning going full blast. For such service, Avis generally charges a $50 membership fee, but it is free for customers identified as potentially profitable. This approach lays the groundwork for future loyalty returns to your company.

Cater to Attractive Segments

Why charge all customers for something not everyone wants or offer a package not everyone needs? Just as bundling can give your company a competitive advantage in building satisfaction and loyalty, so can unbundling. Court and colleagues (1999) refer to this approach as "deaveraging." If customers are allowed to create their own bundles, you send a strong message that you value their business and are concerned about their profitability and success.

Bundling and unbundling are not the only ways to create unique customer offerings, of course. As noted previously, think about building loyalty from the beginning—in the design phase of new offerings or improvements—so that you precisely meet the different needs of various segments. This is the flip side of understanding customers so you can provide them with *unique products* or services. Instead, understand *unique customers* and then offer the bundle of products and services they want, even if the products or services themselves are not unique.

Reach Multiple Segments through Flanking.

Churn indicates that a rival is eroding your customer base. Perhaps the competition has carved out a niche in your customer base that can be penetrated. If it works for them, it can work for you.

All too often, companies think only in terms of price flanking, but there may be opportunities to flank on product or service characteristics. For example, consider adding a high-margin option to a basic offering. The niche market may not be large in absolute numbers, but it can be quite profitable.

Help Employees Build Loyalty

We have just pointed out that employees contribute to customer satisfaction and the experience of value, and the same is true for loyalty. Here are some ways to help them contribute.

Engage Everyone

At Intuit, the chief executive officer periodically spends a few hours on the customer service phones, and the founder of Federated Department Stores often shopped his own stores anonymously. But the involvement of top management is not enough: The insights they gain must be translated into meaningful ways to build customer loyalty. When Bob Pittman, chief executive officer of Six Flags Entertainment, spent a day working as a janitor in one of the parks, he saw customers who were unhappy with the surly janitors they encountered (Heskitt et al. 1994). The employees thought they were just doing their job, which the visitors made harder by making a mess. Pittman felt that changing this attitude could increase customer satisfaction and loyalty. He reframed the task and told janitors their main job was to make sure people had a great time, and a clean park made the experience more enjoyable.

Loyal Employees Mean Loyal Customers

To experience a sense of job satisfaction, employees need to feel that they can meet customer needs. MCI found a direct relationship between employee satisfaction and both customer satisfaction and the intention to stay with MCI (Heskitt et al. 1994). An insurance company study revealed that when service workers left the company, customer satisfaction levels dropped significantly. The SIFO study cited previously reached similar conclusions: The more satisfied employees felt, the better customers felt about Swedbank. Empowered employees are vitally important in providing customer satisfaction as well as in developing customer loyalty.

Tie Compensation to Customer Loyalty

Although product managers and sales personnel are in a key position to create and implement loyalty programs, their compensation packages are rarely tied to retention. If this factor is included in the calculation, your company can send a powerful internal message that attracting customers is not the only thing you value. And point out that it is much less expensive to retain customers than to find new ones.

Create Multiple Contact Points

Various customers need different things in order to feel good about your company. Some prefer face-to-face meetings with salespeople, and others want to interact with help desks or online technicians. One customer likes to visit your Web site for information about your new software, and another prefers an on-site tutorial.

It may appear economical to limit the ways customers may contact your employees, but consider the costs of customer defections. It is worth finding out the kind of contact points valued by a wide range of customers in a long-term relationship with your company, especially as you introduce new and improved products that may require more or different types of customer interaction.

Build Word of Mouth

For many companies, the public relations function is a peripheral way to generate goodwill rather than a significant component in building loyalty. As communication among customers becomes easier and more frequent, and as the information world continues to shrink, public relations can be used effectively to enhance a company's reputation or can present a real threat to loyalty if not managed carefully.

Apostles and Terrorists

For years, Xerox has worked to create "apostles," or people who will preach the company's virtues to others, including potential customers. It also has specific programs to deal with "terrorists," or people who might harm its reputation. With the proliferation of Internet communication, these programs have become even more important (Court et al. 1999).

Most large companies have a public relations department, and coping with disaster is not its only purpose. Have you consulted yours lately to find new ways to build on all your other marketing efforts? Public relations can be inexpensively integrated into a loyalty-building plan, but the department in your company may need a nudge and adequate lead time to make this happen.

Make Lemonade from Lemons

Several years ago, AT&T was faced with an embarrassing situation. Because of problems in several of the most heavily used "switches" (network computers), the service to frame relay users was disrupted for more than a day. The situation could have become a nightmare, but C. Michael Armstrong, Chairman of the Board, stepped in to deal with customers who were experiencing outages. He informed them that there would be no billing, not just for the outage period but until AT&T could understand what happened, fix the problems, and guarantee they would not recur.

Armstrong made it so clear that he was on the customers' side that frame relay users felt more loyalty to AT&T after the event than before. A bad situation with high potential for more negative fallout was turned into a public relations and marketing success. The key is to act quickly and in such a way that customers believe their ongoing business is vitally important to you.

Do Not Oversell

Whether you are building a long-term relationship with a corporate giant or a small business, one of the fastest ways to lose a customer is to oversell your product or service. You may be quite successful in the short run, but long-term relationships cannot be built on false promises. Loyalty and continuity always depend on matching the claims and benefits to what you can deliver.

Pay Attention to Timing

The length of time a customer stays with you can provide valuable insights into what prevented loyalty. The following are some approaches for analyzing the timing of defection.

How Long Did They Stay?

For many products or services, even in the business-to-business arena, retention is computed not in years but in months or even days. A customer who defects after 30 days probably has a different experience than one who is loyal for 12 months. Perhaps claims were made that the product did not fulfill, or benefits did not match need.

A customer who stays a little longer—60 to 90 days—may have responded to a tempting offer that expired, such as a limited period of free financing or free usage. A customer who lasts only to the first renewal date is likely to have found a cheaper option or some problem, perhaps due to inappropriate use or a flaw that emerged. Each type of "loyalty destroyer" requires a different solution, as charted in Exhibit 9-2, which also shows three stages of defection.

Did They Leave Recently?

Recent defectors may be easier to turn around than customers lost months or years earlier. A system that red-flags unhappy customers—before they turn to a competitor—can bring them back into the fold and even strengthen your relationship with them.

Are You Anticipating the Product Life Cycle?

Companies sometimes feel compelled to abandon a market position even when they have loyal customers. They reason that

EXHIBIT 9-2
Defection Stages and Possible Causes and Responses

	Acquisition Stage (1–30 days)	Capture Stage (31–90 days)	Relationship Management Stage (After 90 days)
What went wrong?	False promises— hard sell backfired.	Promotion is over; do not really need/want product.	Could not learn to use, did not use much, or found a cheaper option.
How to build the relationship?	Call customer 1–2 days after sale to thank, offer custom options.	Educate the customer on use, price/value ratio.	Stay in touch with customer through Web site, newsletters, etc. Use feedback to improve.
How to create barriers to exit?	Custom options create sense of involvement.	Follow up after first bill to address specific problems.	Incentive programs, such as point systems, that build loyalty.
How to create flawless customer interactions?	Personal interaction by telephone, e-mail, education, and Web site, whichever is most appropriate.		

decline is inevitable, so they avoid investing any more resources in the product or service. Business-to-business companies should take inspiration from consumer product marketers. Procter & Gamble refuses to let Ivory Soap die: New, improved, reformulated, retextured, repositioned, repackaged, and targeting-refined versions have kept the customer franchise going for more than 100 years. Is there a way your company can do something similar?

Sometimes a brand name can be applied to a new product or product category, as IBM did when it moved into computers, or Microsoft did when it embraced the online business. At other times, it may be necessary to "reinvent" yourself by changing product appearance, service delivery systems, or even your company name and/or logo. Maintaining and building on hard-won loyalty can be so valuable that substantial investment to defy the apparent inevitability of the product life cycle is warranted.

Nurture Personal Relationships

Depending on your product or service, industry, and even company style, there are several ways to nurture personal relationships and strengthen loyalty.

Build Multifaceted, Multilevel Relationships

In the 1970s, MGD Graphics Systems Group, a division of Rockwell International, suddenly faced industry erosion. MGD specialized in high-quality advertising printing equipment, particularly for newspapers. Demand plummeted as newspapers went out of business, merged, or began sharing equipment, and it became vital to keep every customer loyal. MGD weathered this storm because of unusual relationships established with customers.

- The MGD president formed a personal relationship with the publisher of almost every major newspaper in the country.
- The executive vice president for sales did the same with the second-tier executives at these newspapers.
- MGD engineers had close contact with the press engineers for every local newspaper.
- MGD marketing staff was always available to their counterparts on newspapers and often shared information and advice with them.

MGD strengthened this network with a new account management plan. Every account was assigned six or seven people who were responsible for keeping relationships alive and well, even if a newspaper was not considering a purchase in the immediate future. Because of this strategy, MGD came to dominate its industry. No competitor could rival the complexity and depth of these long-term relationships.

Focus on Key Customers

Every year Coke's National Account team meets separately with key personnel at each major client company, sometimes in an off-campus setting. The team makes a polished presentation that reviews joint programs during the previous year, highlights the major successes, and quantifies the incremental profit Coke made for the customer. The discussion then turns to issues that need work, which are carefully researched in advance. Coke then presents new programs for consideration.

The whole event is top quality. If there is a retreat, it is at a luxurious site. If there are outside speakers, they are widely known experts. The focus is on one message: "Isn't it great for us to be in business together?" The event itself makes the customer feel good about the relationship. By concentrating on these key customers, Coke builds loyalty where it will pay off the most.

Accentuate the Personal

Data mining and database developments make it possible to personalize relationships with many or even all customers. The best-known programs are in business-to-consumer companies. For example, Amazon.com suggests books of possible interest when you log on; American Express provides a wide variety of customizable "relationship benefits," ranging from frequent flyer miles to preferred seating (for high-value customers) at major golf and tennis tournaments (Court et al. 1999).

Opportunities for these kinds of relationships in business-to-business settings are increasing as computer-based transactions become common. Reorder cues, e-mail announcements of new products or services of particular interest to a customer, and invitations to focus groups or roundtables are some examples. Whether through electronic or print media or face-to-face contact, there are ways to make every customer feel valued and special. It is worth remembering that some customers prefer less contact and information. As you enrich and personalize relationships, keep individual needs and preferences in mind.

Borrow Interest

Borrowing interest to build loyalty can be a valuable tool. The classic case is customer-oriented products, such as frequent flyer programs, but the concept can be used in business-to-business situations and has been for years. The vice president of sales invites the customer's vice president of manufacturing on a golf outing or to a retreat in Palm Springs or Hawaii—when purchases reach a certain level.

Business-to-business companies have much more sophisticated tools at their disposal. Some build "a network of innovative partners" (Court et al. 1999). For example, an equipment manufacturer partners with a financial institution that can lend funds to a customer interested in making a major capital purchase. The manufacturer can close a sale, and both partners develop a relationship with the customer, who may return to the bank for other loans. An alliance or even an acquisition can help you put together a unique package that differentiates your offering and rewards customer loyalty.

Other approaches may require creativity or individuation. For example, a small accounting firm in Taos, N.Mex., which serves local and regional businesses with no single account worth more than $50,000 a year, invites a few carefully selected customers to its annual Christmas party. The source of borrowed interest is the setting, the best restaurant in Taos, where the menu is an original seasonal special that the restaurant premiers at this party, supplemented by wines from an excellent local vineyard.

Focus on Customers Who Can Be Loyal

Not every customer for every product or service can be loyal, regardless of incentives. Analyze situations with this in mind to be sure you use your marketing investment effectively. Loyalty is easier to achieve in two cases: (1) customers have few options, and (2) customers value relationships and prefer to avoid switching.

Loyalty is severely threatened but still possible in these two cases: (1) when significant changes occur in an industry, such as technological advances, that shake the strongest customer loyalty (Blattberg and Deighton 1996) and (2) when the competitive picture changes dramatically. New entrants offer new options or new relationships that tempt loyal customers. In these cases, you need to rethink the game before you can expect to build customer loyalty, regardless of how strong loyalty has been in the past.

In some situations, it is so difficult or expensive to build loyalty that this goal may not be worth pursuing. There may be so many substitutes for your offering that customers in effect experience no switching barriers or penalties, no matter what you do. Long-distance services have faced this challenge for several years. Or, uncertainty in the marketplace makes customers reluctant to commit over the long run. In many industries, for example, the Internet has created turmoil in old ways of doing business. Also, as noted previously, some customers are required by law to use a bidding process.

If loyalty simply is not in the cards for your company at this point, that only means you need to invest more time and energy in refining your approach to the other steps in the CLC to attract and serve a more loyalty-prone customer base.

Attack Churn Directly

If churn is the major indicator of a loyalty problem for your company, launch an integrated program focused on turnover. Its components will vary according to the defection stage, or how recently the customer was lost (see Exhibit 9-2). Within each stage, you can design specific programs to build the relationship, create barriers to exit for that customer, offer flawless customer service, and back all this up with excellent, preferably unique products. Examples of actions to combat churn are given in Exhibit 9-3.

E-COMMERCE AND LOYALTY

Electronic technologies can be both a blessing and a curse to marketers trying to build customer loyalty. On the positive side, databases can open up vast opportunities to develop deep knowledge about customers, their needs, and their reactions to your programs. On the negative side, the turmoil created in many industries by e-commerce will be felt for years to come. Because it takes time to implement computer-based systems for tracking, understanding, and managing customers, even approaches that may not be right for your company today are worth considering for the future. Time also may be needed to win internal approval.

Most companies are not accustomed to think about large start-up costs in the marketing area, and payback on expenditures is expected within a year or two at the most. In the case of e-commerce, as business-to-consumer companies have demonstrated, it can be very expensive to set up the system, and the breakeven point can occur well into the future. For example, Amazon.com estimates 12 years for some of its investments in building a customer base (Kenny and Marshall 2000). Equally dramatic, however, is the low cost of serving a loyal e-commerce purchaser, which translates into high profit margins.

Therefore, two factors regarding loyalty come into play. First, a loyal customer can generate substantial profits for your company. Second, the faster your e-commerce offering can attract and hold new customers, the faster you will reap profits.

Perhaps surprisingly, customers who purchase on the Web are less likely to use multiple suppliers than are those who buy through traditional channels. The reason is unclear. It may be that they are reluctant to spend time learning about multiple sites and transaction requirements or that few suppliers have a strong e-commerce offering (Reichheld and Schefter 2000). At least for now, it appears that moving customers to an e-commerce relationship can itself increase loyalty.

Another important point is that word of mouth, or in e-commerce terms, word of mouse, is particularly powerful among e-commerce users. Online buyers are more likely than traditional purchasers to provide referrals, both to the sellers with whom

EXHIBIT 9-3
Four Ways to Attack Churn

The Four Loyalty Levers	Defection in Acquisition Stage (1–30 days)	Defection in Capture Stage (31–90 days)	Defection in Relationship Management Stage (after 90 days)
Build the relationship.	Use preferential selection to focus on best customers.	Educate customers on how to experience value.	Create specific "win back" programs that target defections.
Create barriers to exit.	Offer incentives to invest in your technology.	Use promotions to stimulate usage.	Use promotions to encourage continuity.
Provide flawless customer service.	Maintain "aggressive" customer contact.	Handle billing, service, and returns promptly and effectively.	Conduct surveys and act on the findings.
Offer excellent products.	Offer products or upgrades with unique capabilities and/or customize products.	Provide top-quality technical support.	Get customer involved in product development.

they deal (about potential customers) and to other buyers (about specific sellers) (Reichheld and Schefter 2000). This aspect of loyalty has the additional value of reducing the cost of acquiring customers.

Kenny and Marshall (2000) provide fascinating insights into where e-commerce may be headed over the next few years. Here are some that are relevant to loyalty:

1. E-commerce will reach buyers wherever they are and whatever they are doing through "contextual marketing." For business-to-business companies, that may translate into an extension of approaches already in place, such as a terminal in the customer's mail room that allows the clerk to connect directly with FedEx for package addressing, pricing, and pick-up.

2. Customers will no longer be required to go to seller sites to transact business. Rather, companies will "borrow" information on customers so that they can make offers in the context in which customers may want to purchase, such as advertisements for Tylenol on e-broker sites that appear only when the stock market is falling. By reaching customers when they are predisposed to buy, the seller creates a high potential for future loyalty because the approach demonstrates that buyer and seller are in harmony and presents the seller in a less cluttered competitive arena.

3. E-commerce will make it so easy for customers to do business with one supplier that they will become loyal almost by default. Even for a million-dollar purchase, ease of access to information may be the deciding factor if the buyer can check instantly on how manufacturing, shipping, or installation is progressing and plan accordingly.

Information abounds about e-commerce as a loyalty builder. Court and colleagues (1999) discuss creating online user groups and online access at new levels. *McKinsey Quarterly Online* (2001) notes that gross margins, operating margins, revenues, and loyalty measures such as repeat usage increase for highly successful e-commerce companies. Articles in traditional business journals and e-commerce publications such as *Wired* and *eCompany Now* maintain that the e-seller addresses the real needs of buyers, and that is perhaps the strongest loyalty-builder of all.

SUMMARY OF STEP EIGHT: BUILDING LOYALTY

Loyalty must be assessed by looking at customers' actions, not just intent. Although loyalty and satisfaction are closely related, they are not synonymous. Loyalty refers to a relationship over time, whereas satisfaction is a function of customer experience at one point in time.

The definition of loyalty varies by business, by industry, and whether the offering is a product or service. Repurchase, retention, relationship strength, and other factors can all play a part in the definition of loyalty for an individual product or service. Because the meaning varies, the measure of loyalty reflects each business situation. Ask the right questions, decide in advance how to define loyalty and exactly what to measure, gather timely information, and focus on the right customers.

There are many effective approaches to building loyalty. Offer a unique product or service, segment the market from the loyalty point of view, use public relations approaches, pay attention to the timing of defections, nurture personal relationships, borrow interest, concentrate on the right customers, and attack churn directly.

E-commerce can build loyalty and will be increasingly effective in the future. A company that does not integrate e-commerce into its total business approach risks being left behind in a period of rapidly changing customer expectations.

Chapter 10

How to Create Profits from Marketing Chaos

The Customer Learning Curve helps you conquer and capitalize on marketing chaos in two ways. First, the eight steps are specific guidelines for gaining a deeper understanding of your customers. Second, the mathematical model identifies key leverage points for influencing customer experiences, which maximizes return on marketing expenditures. This chapter explains how to apply the CLC to your unique marketing situation, but before we begin, some information about the model will be useful.

The CLC was developed in response to a company's need to convert its large annual investment in excellent market research into actions and improved performance. The CLC model mapped many of the research results into strategic insights about how to move customers along the path from need to loyalty. It also helped measure marketing effectiveness. Even for organizations that already use market research to great advantage, the CLC is a framework for comparing marketing investments and assessing effectiveness.

Consult Exhibit 10-1 to see how studies and internal data can be mapped into the strategic context of the CLC. The exhibit can be used in at least three ways. First, if you know the leverage point (CLC step) at which most of your prospects encounter a barrier, that column in the exhibit is a guide for measuring that step. Second, if you have conducted or are planning a particular type of market research, look in the lower sections of the exhibit to see where this kind of research is often helpful. Third, your research archives can be organized by using the exhibit as a guide to the relevance of each study.

GETTING STARTED

Your mission is to close the gap between potential (total market for your offerings) and penetration (total sales for your offering), and numerical measures indicate your programs' effectiveness. If you do not begin by thinking about the size of your potential market, you cannot decide whether money should be spent to increase market share or dominate the market or whether you should withdraw from a market too small to justify your investment. And you will have no baseline from which to measure progress if you do not identify your current sales rate, or penetration. Exhibit 10-2 illustrates the relationship between potential and penetration as these terms are used in the CLC.

Fill in the parameters you already know. If you know the close rate of your sales force, use it to estimate the number of customers who make it through Step Five (purchase). If you track churn, pinpoint the problem. A customer may defect in Step Six (know-how), Step Seven (experience value), or Step Eight (loyalty). Churn indicates the total number of customers who leave after purchase. If you work with an advertising agency, request market research to measure the percentage of your target customers who can restate your product or service's points of difference and use this percentage for Step Two, awareness.

Now use the CLC model to estimate the percentages for which you do not have hard numbers. These estimates become hypotheses to validate in the next steps of investigation. If they stand the test of logic and available facts, they become baseline levels against which you can both project desired program outcomes and measure progress after you implement changes.

An example in a typical business-to-business setting is Aries Software, the company described in Chapter 1. It has moved forward in time five years, and Samantha Hathaway, Vice President of Marketing, knows that sales (penetration) last year were $23 million. Her market research team recently resurveyed the market and estimates that each year companies will spend $650 million on the kind of software Aries sells (potential). About half of them (55%) have needs that can be met exactly by the package Aries has put together. Hathaway's first entries into the CLC model are shown in Exhibit 10-3.

Hathaway also knows the close rate of her salespeople. In 60% of situations in which the sales force provides a bid to a potential buyer, Aries makes a sale. Although Aries originally sold

EXHIBIT 10-1
The Gap Between Potential and Penetration

Potential   **Where the CLC Numbers Come From**

NEED	AWARE	ACCESS	MOTIVATE
Main Measure: Percentage of *potential* customers who need your product, whether they know it or not. Includes current and competitive customers.	**Main Measure:** Percentage of prospects who need product and know about yours and why they should buy it instead of an alternative.	**Main Measure:** Percentage of prospects who need and are aware of your product and who can access it.	**Main Measure:** Percentage of prospects who need, are aware, have access, and intend to purchase.
Key Strategic Issue: Market segmentation. Different customers need different benefits. To serve two segments with a single marketing strategy misses at least one and probably both.	**Key Strategic Issue:** Positioning. Target knows difference from competitors and proof of it; name of product. Especially for mature products, your mantra must be differentiate or die.	**Key Strategic Issue:** Potentially four—wrong channel; product not deployed in prospect's area; inadequate know-how to take advantage of product; blocked by a competitive relationship.	**Key Strategic Issue:** Is product important enough for intrinsic motivation to work? If not, what does target care about (from which I can borrow interest)?
Think Hard Questions: Whose demand is met by my supplying my product? What are the possible benefits of my product? What are the characteristics of those who would value it? How can I count them? Who will I reach practically (targets)?	**Think Hard Questions:** Who are my targets? How can I get my message to them? What is the one thing I want prospects to know about my product? How can I educate, not just create superficial awareness?	**Think Hard Questions:** How does customer prefer accessing my product? Do other companies (channels) add value to my product? What does the customer need to know to get value from my product? Can I trump or go around a competitive relationship?	**Think Hard Questions:** Why are targets not buying my product? How can I offer a free sample? What do my targets care about?
Ways to Get Numbers and Strategic Insights: Focus groups or qualitative interviews on how customers might benefit from your product (yin/expansive research) Forums with "bell cow" users to expand market definition. Survey your own and competitors' customers (yang/focused research) Create profiles: 1. Firmographics—Industry, size, geography 2. Life cycle stage and attitudes toward innovation 3. Approach to purchasing: transaction or alliance 4. Profile of buyer Intent-to-purchase question:* •All the definitely's and half the probably's estimate size of prime targets (yang). •Ask "why did you answer as you did?" to widen your target (yin). Data Mining: Capture large flows of information through Internet, customer service, sales, and so on, and create usage profiles.	**Ways to Get Numbers and Strategic Insights:** Survey target customers •Measure recall of advertisements and brand awareness as a base. •Measure knowledge of your value proposition. Sample question: 1. Unprompted: *If you had (a problem or application need) how would you address it?* (include your product in list of answers) 2. Prompted follow-up: *What about (your product)? How well would this product address the need? Excellent, very well, well, or poorly? Why did you answer as you did?* Conduct awareness-building experiments—test combinations of awareness-building tools and measure effect—pre- and posttests, control group.	**Ways to Get Numbers and Strategic Insights:** If channels are relevant: What proportion stocks, recommends, promotes my product? What do channel members care about? How can I fit in? If deployment is relevant (as for phone companies): What percentage of target am I capable of serving? Where is highest density of targets for next investment? If know-how is relevant: What percentage of target has comparable technology or practices? If relationship blockage is relevant: In what percentage of targets is competitor embedded? Open communication up and down the channel to examine sources of value, flows of information, product, and money.	**Ways to Get Numbers and Strategic Insights:** Survey target customers: Intent-to-purchase question:* •Describe your product's value proposition and ask likelihood of purchase at price x: Definitely, probably, maybe, probably not, definitely not. •Ask why they responded as they did. Focus groups or qualitative interviews with nonbuyers: Why didn't you buy? What extra value would get you to buy? How about (a proposed promotion)? Conduct marketing experiments—test markets—to learn what motivates customers and how competitors react.

EXHIBIT 10-1
Continued

Where the CLC Numbers Come From

Penetration

PURCHASE KNOW-HOW EXPERIENCE VALUE RETAIN

Main Measure: Percentage of motivated prospects who have purchased.	**Main Measure:** Percentage of customers who can use all the features they want to.	**Main Measure:** Overall rating of value for dollar paid.	**Main Measure:** Percentage of customers who plan to buy again.

Key Strategic Issue: Pricing and sales force effectiveness	**Key Strategic Issue:** Educate about product use. Are customers getting all the productivity they can from it? What do they need to know to do better?	**Key Strategic Issue:** Create value for the customer and capture some of it for my company?	**Key Strategic Issue:** Preferential selection and the four loyalty levers—product uniqueness, service excellence, barriers to exit, and relationship
Think Hard Questions: The five C's of pricing—customers, competitors, cost, control, and change.			
How effective is my sales force? Are they calling on the right people? Do they deliver my message? Are they credible? Are they rewarded appropriately? What percent do they close?	**Think Hard Questions:** What is the usage situation? Is my product easy to use? What do customers need to know? How can I teach them? How could education become a point of difference for me?	**Think Hard Questions:** How can I increase customer satisfaction? Redesign my product? Augment it with service? Can I execute better? Is my price right?	**Think Hard Questions:** Am I attracting the wrong customers—ones who are bound to leave? How can I increase satisfaction among the right customers? How can I create barriers to exit? Can I motivate increased usage? Can I create continuity programs?
Ways to Get Numbers and Strategic Insights: Conjoint analysis: •Market share and revenue effects of alternative benefit bundles at alternative prices •Benefit segmentation •Likely competitive responses to your pricing moves	**Ways to Get Numbers and Strategic Insights:** Survey target customers: •rate the ease of use of each aspect of your product. •"Would you use this feature if it were easier to use?"	**Ways to Get Numbers and Strategic Insights:** Customer satisfaction surveys of at least three groups: The dissatisfied, from whom you learn what must be fixed; the very satisfied, from whom you learn what to preserve; and the lukewarm, from whom you learn what else you must do.	**Ways to Get Numbers and Strategic Insights:** Internal measures of churn: Track lost customers and investigate a sample to find out why they left and identify patterns.
Internal measure: Sales force close rate, monitor pipeline			
Survey target customers who recently had contact with your sales force. Ask: Did you get a presentation? Was it compelling? Credible? If you bought, what influenced you? If not, why not?	Focus groups or qualitative interviews with customers to develop ways to make your product easier to use and to educate customers.	Conjoint analysis helps fine tune your product and your price for greater value.	Focus groups with loyal users to find how to share their practices with "average" customers and develop continuity programs.
Focus groups with salespeople:	Focus groups of customer service people: What are the patterns of problems? What are simplification or education opportunities?	Gap analysis identifies ways to improve your product.	Track success of loyalty and continuity programs: How happy are your best customers with them? How could they be better?
•why the top 5% succeed •what the next 35% need to do better		Correlate internal measures on satisfaction and loyalty so you can predict performance and make course corrections.	
Conduct sales program experiments—program A to region 1, and program B to region 2.	Observation: Watch customers use your product on site		Survey dissatisfied customers and ask: How well did we respond? Survey loyal customers and ask: What are we doing right? Survey lukewarm customers with a concept test of loyalty builders.
	Engage customers in Internet dialogues.	Use technology to sense customer experience—voice response system wait time, video on-site usage of products, real-time dialogue through Internet.	
Use technology to increase speed of information on sales response.	Conduct customer education experiments.		Conduct continuity building experiments.

*The answer to the intent-to-purchase question will provide insights into prospects' reasons for getting stuck at this step of the CLC.

EXHIBIT 10-2
The Gap Between Potential and Penetration

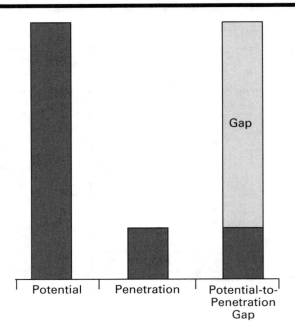

Potential   Penetration   Potential-to-
Penetration
Gap

EXHIBIT 10-3
Initial Information on Aries Software

Potential = $650 million.

NEED › AWARE › ACCESS › MOTIVATE › PURCHASE › KNOW-HOW › EXPERIENCE VALUE › RETAIN

55%   =

$357.5
million $23
million

Penetration = $23 million.

its product online, it eventually moved to direct sales exclusively. Hathaway adds the 60% figure, as indicated in Exhibit 10-4.

Hathaway has even more figures she can enter. Because Aries hires an advertising agency that works hard to keep the account, the agency conducts annual market research to measure awareness among potential customers. The figure last year was 45%, which is added to the model in Exhibit 10-5.

Hathaway next supplies the five missing percentages by estimating what they must be, assuming for the moment that they are equal and that they make the rest of the numbers in the model fit together. This process is called *forcing*. (Some managers set up an Excel spreadsheet and use trial and error to find the right percentages. Those with algebra skill will recognize an equation in which the missing value is the fifth root of the other values properly manipulated—in general, the nth root, where n equals the number of missing percentages. Or use the interactive model for the Curve at www.resultrek.com.) The resulting CLC is given in Exhibit 10-6.

When you translate Hathaway's experience to your situation, whether you create a spreadsheet or use the interactive CLC model, there are three important things to remember. First, estimates are acceptable at this point. Perhaps you do not have current information on awareness, need, or other aspects. Rather

EXHIBIT 10-4
Close Rate Information for Aries Software at the Purchase Stage

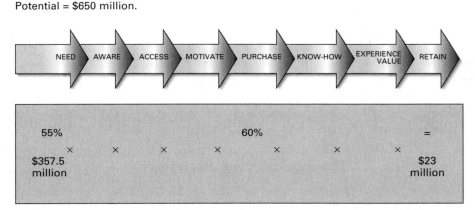

Potential = $650 million.

| NEED | AWARE | ACCESS | MOTIVATE | PURCHASE | KNOW-HOW | EXPERIENCE VALUE | RETAIN |

55%				60%			=
×	×	×	×	×	×	×	
$357.5 million							$23 million

Penetration = $23 million.

EXHIBIT 10-5
Awareness Information on Aries Software

Potential = $650 million.

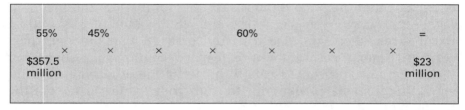

Penetration = $23 million.

than omit these elements, put them into the model for now as a starting point. Second, the mathematical model will work with any number of entries as long as you have the first and the last figures. The point is to start somewhere, with whatever information you have. Third, there is a small trick to using the model: The percentage shown under each step is the number that yielded the unit or dollar amount for that step. When the dollars that made it through the previous step are multiplied by this percentage, the result is the dollars that make it through this step. For example, when Hathaway used the 45% awareness level to determine the dollar sales to customers who both need her product and are aware of its benefit, she multiplied $357.5 million (spent by those who need her product) by 45% (the aware portion of the target audience) to arrive at $160.9 million (the amount spent by those who have both need and awareness). Exhibit 10-7 illustrates the process.

REFINING THE NUMBERS

You can refine the numbers in the CLC model to determine marketing leverage in your particular business situation. Market research is the best tool, but it may not be available. In this case,

EXHIBIT 10-6
Aries CLC with Estimated (Forced) Values

Potential = $650 million.

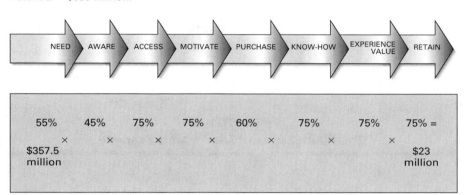

| NEED | AWARE | ACCESS | MOTIVATE | PURCHASE | KNOW-HOW | EXPERIENCE VALUE | RETAIN |

55%	45%	75%	75%	60%	75%	75%	75% =
×	×	×	×	×	×	×	
$357.5 million							$23 million

Penetration = $23 million.

talk to departments in your organization. In most business-to-business companies, information through Step Five (from need through purchase) is obtained from the marketing and sales functions, and the remainder (know-how, value experience, and loyalty) is the responsibility of customer service functions.

At Aries Software, Hathaway learns from the customer service group that each year 30% of customers who purchase software either return it or do not extend its use to another part of their business in which it would be applicable. In other words, the churn rate is 30%, and 70% of customers do not defect. This new information means that the product of the last three percentages must be 70%. If these percentages are equal, each is 89% (89% × 89% × 89% = 70%). So Hathaway replaces the old forced figure of 75% with 89% in each of the last three steps of her CLC.

Then customer service tells Hathaway that most of the churn results from returns within 30 days of purchase. This indicates that know-how is a more significant factor in defections than value or loyalty issues. With this in mind, Hathaway revises her figures: 73% for know-how, 98% for value, and 98% for loyalty (73% × 98% × 98% = 70%). In marketing terms, Aries lost customers because they could not learn how to use the software. But those who did learn liked it and were loyal to it.

The change in the last three percentages put the CLC out of balance mathematically, so Hathaway went back to two other forced numbers, access and motivation. If these were equal, they would need to be 58% each to make all the numbers fit together. In Hathaway's marketing judgment, access was slightly better than motivation: She chose 65% for the former and 52% for the latter. Her CLC draft at this point is given in Exhibit 10-8.

EXHIBIT 10-7
The Multiplication "Trick": Aries Example

Potential = $650 million.

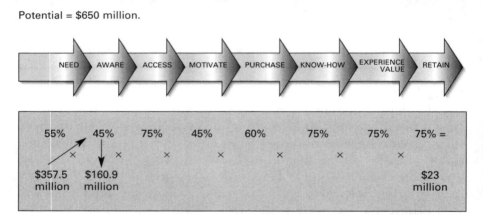

Penetration = $23 million.

In General:

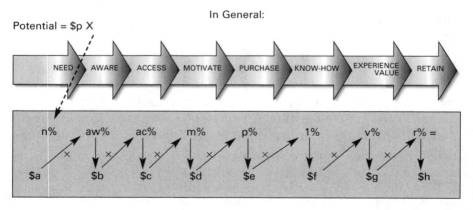

Penetration = $h.

In summary thus far, create such a draft for yourself by putting in the numbers you know and using a spreadsheet or the interactive model to fill in forced numbers where needed. Then make adjustments based on your experience. Because our Web tool is so easy to use, this should be relatively painless, even if you make three, four, or even more alterations.

MAKING PROGRAMMATIC CHOICES

With the basic mathematics behind you, marketing creativity comes into play. Look at your CLC and identify areas that lend themselves to strategic marketing intervention. This is what Hathaway did. She started by looking at what she seemed to be doing right: Value and loyalty figures were high. Less work was needed in these areas. Then she noted the lower figure for need, but raising that number would require major product development, an investment her company was not in a position to make. In your case, find the highest numbers, or areas in which you are already successful, and identify areas in which improvement is prohibitively expensive. Put a low priority on brainstorming about interventions in these steps, at least temporarily.

Next, Hathaway looked at the lowest numbers to see which represented the greatest opportunities. Her lows were: 45%

EXHIBIT 10-8
Refining the Numbers

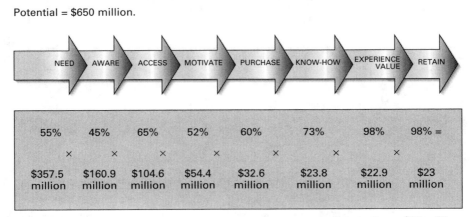

Potential = $650 million.

NEED	AWARE	ACCESS	MOTIVATE	PURCHASE	KNOW-HOW	EXPERIENCE VALUE	RETAIN
55%	45%	65%	52%	60%	73%	98%	98% =
×	×	×	×	×	×	×	
$357.5 million	$160.9 million	$104.6 million	$54.4 million	$32.6 million	$23.8 million	$22.9 million	$23 million

Penetration = $23 million.

aware, 52% motivated, 60% purchase, 65% access, and 73% know-how. What if she could increase awareness, the very lowest, from 45% to 60%? How would that affect revenue?

Hathaway adjusted the percentage using the Web model and created a "what if" chart, shown in Exhibit 10-9. Aries had a margin of 60%, and the awareness increase yielded $7.5 million in incremental revenue, or $4.5 million in additional margin. If an advertising program to raise awareness costs $1 million, it would return 4.5 times its cost in margin and 7.5 times its cost in revenue. If Hathaway's assumptions were correct, this clearly represented an attractive option. She decided to design specific programs and use market research to determine whether the programs would generate the revenue she predicted.

You can go through this same exercise and create "what if" charts for your lowest figure. You also can use the model to see what happens if you raise two or three of the lowest numbers. This activity provides (1) inspiration, from seeing how much improvement is available; (2) focus, by putting the relative effect of changes in each step in perspective; and (3) estimates of poten-

EXHIBIT 10-9
What If Awareness Rose from 45% to 60%?

Potential = $650 million.

NEED	AWARE	ACCESS	MOTIVATE	PURCHASE	KNOW-HOW	EXPERIENCE VALUE	RETAIN
55%	45% ↓ 60% ×	65%	52%	60%	73%	98%	98% =
$357.5 million	$214.5 million	$139.4 million	$72.5 million	$43.5 million	$31.8 million	$31.1 million	$30.5 million

Penetration moves from $23 million to $30.5 million.
Result: $7.5 million in incremental revenue, or a 33% increase.
At 60% margin, this represents $4.5 million in incremental margin.

tial returns, which provide rough guidelines for thinking about marketing investments.

You are now in a position to make choices. Your CLC analysis indicates programs that will substantially increase revenues, and the kind of computations described above enable you to compare their costs and benefits. Exhibit 10-10 is a chart Hathaway prepared for comparative purposes. She wanted to know whether to launch an awareness campaign or invest $500,000 in sales training to raise the close rate to 75% in the purchase stage. This option would generate an additional $3.4 million in profits, or a return of $6.70 of margin for each marketing dollar, compared

EXHIBIT 10-10
What If the Close Rate Rose from 60% to 75%?

Potential = $650 million.

NEED	AWARE	ACCESS	MOTIVATE	PURCHASE	KNOW-HOW	EXPERIENCE VALUE	RETAIN

55%	45%	65%	52%	60%	73%	98%	98% =
				↓			
				75%			
×	×	×	×	×	×	×	
$357.5 million	$160.9 million	$104.6 million	$54.4 million	$32.6	$23.8	$22.9	$23
				↓	↓	↓	↓
				$40.8 million	$29.8 million	$29.2 million	$28.6 million

Penetration moves from $23 million
↓
to $28.6 million.

Result: $5.6 million in incremental revenue.

At 60% margin, this represents $3.4 million in incremental margin.

Return on marketing investment: $3.4 million ÷ $500,000 =

6.70 margin to expense ratio.

with \$4.50 for the awareness-building program. She decided that the sales training would be better.

When you use the CLC model to calculate the marketing return of program options, you need to estimate the "sales response function," or the effect of implementing a program. Your own marketing history may be helpful in determining a marketing program's effectiveness: "We tried this program last year and the result was x." Even better are product or service trials or test markets, because you can control the program, measure the results, and learn in greater detail. Another option is market research concept tests, which are much less expensive than full-scale test markets and provide some basis for estimating the effects of alternative programs. If there is no relevant history, and market research is too costly, draw on the experience of key salespeople, your advertising agency, and other marketers in your company. Measure carefully as you implement programs and keep records to use in the future.

SUMMARY OF THE PROCEDURE

Application of the CLC model to your situation may seem complicated, but the approach is straightforward.

1. *Put the numbers you have*, whether firm or best estimates, into the CLC model. Using the Web tool or your own calculations, *estimate the missing numbers*, if any.
2. *Refine the numbers*, on the basis of your judgment and experience with your product or service. *Rerun the numbers* to get a revised best estimate.
3. *Identify the greatest opportunities*. Ignore the CLC steps for which your numbers are already high or intervention is too expensive, and focus on the low numbers.
4. *Choose one CLC step* for a possible intervention and *rerun the model* with an estimate of feasible improvements due to that change.
5. *Brainstorm programs* that might improve your numbers, and make *rough cost estimates* for them.
6. *Compute the potential profit contribution* of each program, and *compare the profit increase to program cost*.
7. *Repeat* the last three calculations for other CLC steps, programs, or combinations of programs, and *select the option(s)* most suitable for your situation.

MAKING THE CLC A REALITY IN YOUR ORGANIZATION

The CLC provides insight, logic, and financial analysis, all critically important contributions to your ability to put your organization on a successful path forward. The ancient Chinese sages not only developed the concept of yin and yang to explain how the world works but also understood the fundamental components of leadership. Some of their observations are relevant to the challenge of guiding your company in its quest for breakthrough business results.

Zen Lessons: The Art of Leadership (Cleary 1989) suggests three essentials of leadership: humanity, clarity, and courage. If all three are present, the community—or the company—flourishes. If one or more is lacking, prospects are poor. From the perspective of corporate managers, the CLC contributes to all three.

Humanity pertains to what benefits everyone in the company. The humanity aspect of the CLC is its ability to create consensus based on a common, fact-based understanding, communicated in a common language that reduces the conflicts of marketing decision making. In leading your organization to embrace the CLC as an effective management tool, you must point out its basic benefit to everyone in the company.

Clarity is inherent in the CLC's unique elements of mathematical analysis and structured thinking from the customer's point of view. The approach can help managers at every level have a clearer perspective on the realities of the current marketplace.

Courage is no different now than in the era of the Chinese sages. It means standing behind your convictions and walking your talk. The CLC helps strengthen your convictions by identifying what you know, what you do not know, and the implications of various actions. This knowledge gives you the courage to lead.

The CLC presents an opportunity for growth and change. Here is a tool that is dynamic, flexible, and powerful. Here is a way not only to resolve marketing chaos but also to turn it into profits for your company and a better future for all the products and services you offer.

References

Blattberg, Robert and John Deighton (1996), "Manage Marketing by the Customer Equity Test," *Harvard Business Review*, 74 (July/August), 136–44.

Cleary, Thomas, trans. (1989), *Zen Lessons: The Art of Leadership*. Boston and London: Shambhala Publications.

Court, David, Thomas D. French, Tim I. McGuire, and Michael Partington (1999), "Marketing in 3-D," *McKinsey Quarterly Online*, (accessed January 31, 2003), [available at http://www.mckinseyquarterly.com/article_page.asp?tk=:371:&articlenum=371].

Davenport, Thomas H. and John C. Beck (2000), "Getting the Attention You Need," *Harvard Business Review*, (September/October), 119–26.

Deutsch, Claudia H. (2000), "New Economy, Old-School Rigor," *New York Times*, (June 12), C1.

DeVincentis, John and Neil Rackman (1998), "Breadth of a Salesman," *McKinsey Quarterly Online*, (accessed January 31, 2003), [available at http://www.mckinseyquarterly.com/article_page.asp?articlenum=309].

Edmunds, Holly (1999), *The Focus Group Research Handbook*. Chicago: American Marketing Association and NTC Business Books.

Evans, Philip and Thomas S. Wurster (2000), *Blown to Bits: How the New Economics of Information Transforms Strategy*. Boston: Harvard Business School Press.

Hayashi, Alden M. (2001), "When to Trust Your Gut," *Harvard Business Review*, 79 (February), 59–66.

Heskitt, James L., Thomas O. Jones, Gary W. Loveman, W. Earl Sasser Jr., and Leonard A. Schlesinger (1994), "Putting the Service-Profit Chain to Work," *Harvard Business Review*, 72 (March/April), 164ff.

Intelliquest (1999), *Preference Structure Measurement: Conjoint Analysis and Related Techniques*. Chicago: American Marketing Association.

Johnson, Michael D. and Anders Gustafsson (2000), *Improving Customer Satisfaction, Loyalty and Profit: An Integrated Measurement and Management System*. San Francisco: Jossey-Bass.

Katzenbach, Jon R. (2000), "Five Paths Toward a High-Performing Workforce," *HBS Working Knowledge*, (posted August 21), (accessed March 25, 2003), [available at http://hbsworkingknowledge.hbs.edu/item.jhtml?id=1646&t=organizations].

Kenny, David and John F. Marshall (2000), "Contextual Marketing: The Real Business of the Internet," *Harvard Business Review*, 78 (November/December), 119–25.

Kirkpatrick, David (2000), "Be Like Mike," *eCompanyNow*, (December), 85–86.

Klompmaker, Jay (1991), "Value Positioning Versus Competition," paper presented at Furniture Pricing Strategies to Increase Profit: Putting Value Back in the Furniture Business, The Learning Corporation, Pinehurst, NC (September).

Marconi, Joe (2000), *Future Marketing*. Chicago: American Marketing Association and NTC Business Books.

McKinsey Quarterly Online (2001), "E-Performance: The Path to Rational Exuberance Continued," (accessed January 31, 2003), [available at http://premium.mckinseyquarterly.com/article_page.aspx?ar =975&L2=24&L3=45].

Moore, Geoffrey (1995), *Inside the Tornado: Marketing Strategies from Silicon Valley's Cutting Edge*. New York: HarperCollins.

——— and Regis McKenna (1999), *Crossing the Chasm: Marketing and Selling High-Tech Products to Mainstream Customers*. New York: HarperBusiness.

Mount, Ian (2000), "Ebola. Smallpox. Christina Aguilera. What Do the Above Have in Common? They All Spread Virally," *eCompany Now*, (October), (accessed March 18, 2003), [available at http://www.busi- ness2.com/articles/mag/0,1640,7511,ff.html].

Ogilvie, David (1985), *Ogilvie on Advertising*, 1st Vintage Books Edition. New York: Vintage Books.

Pine, Joe and Jim Gilmore (2000), "The Experience Economy: Work Is Theater and Every Business a Stage," *HBS Working Knowledge*, (accessed January 31, 2003), [available at http://hbswk.hbs.edu/item. jhtml?id=863&t=marketing&sid=0&pid=0].

Quintus Corporation (2000), "Ten Reasons Your Ecommerce Website Needs Live Help," *CRMXchange* (accessed June 28, 2000), [available at].

Rao, Akshay, Mark Bergen, and Scott Davis (2000), "How to Fight a Price War: Analyzing the Battleground," *HBS Working Knowledge*, (accessed January 31, 2003), [available at http://hbswk.hbs.edu/item. jhtml?id=1679&t=marketing&sid=0&pid=0].

Reichheld, Frederick and Phil Schefter (2000), "E-Loyalty: Your Secret Weapon on the Web," *Harvard Business Review*, 78 (October), 125–35.

Rich, Motoko (2000), "Services Companies Set Online Alliance to Purchase Goods," *The Wall Street Journal*, (April 26), A16.

Rogers, Everett M. (1983), *Diffusion of Innovation*, 3d ed. New York: The Free Press.

Smith, Ellen Reid (2000), *e-Loyalty: How to Keep Customers Coming Back to Your Website*. New York: HarperBusiness.

Stern, Louis W. and Frederick D. Sturdivant (1987), "Customer-Driven Distribution Systems," *Harvard Business Review*, 65 (July), 34–41.

Sudman, Seymour and Brian Wansink (2001), *Consumer Panels*, 2d ed. Chicago: American Marketing Association.

Weber, John A. (1986), *Identifying and Solving Marketing Problems with Gap* Analysis. Notre Dame, IN: Strategic Business Systems, as quoted in Kotler, Philip (2000), *Marketing Management*, Millennium Edition. Upper Saddle River, NJ: Prentice Hall.

Whitlaw, Steve (2001), personal telephone interview (August).

Wise, Richard and David Morrison (2000), "Beyond the Exchange: The Future of B2B," *Harvard Business Review*, (November/December), 86–96.

Wright, T.P. (1936), "Learning Curve Calculator," Journal of the Aeronautical Science, (February), (accessed August 31, 2000), [available at http://www.jsc.nasa.gov/bu2/learn.html].

Zaltman, Jerry and Vincent P. Barabba (1991), *Hearing the Voice of the Market: Competitive Advantage Through Creative Use of Market Information*. Boston: Harvard Business School Press.

Index